The Funniest People in
Religion and Families

The Funniest People in Religion and Families

◆

250 Anecdotes About Saints, Sinners, Rabbis, Zen Masters, and More;

And

250 Anecdotes About Children, Husbands and Wives, Couples, Grandparents, Teachers, Pets, and More

David Bruce

iUniverse, Inc.
New York Lincoln Shanghai

The Funniest People in Religion and Families
250 Anecdotes About Saints, Sinners, Rabbis, Zen Masters, and More;

And

250 Anecdotes About Children, Husbands and Wives, Couples, Grandparents, Teachers, Pets, and More

iUniverse books may be ordered through booksellers or by contacting:

iUniverse
2021 Pine Lake Road, Suite 100
Lincoln, NE 68512
www.iuniverse.com
1-800-Authors (1-800-288-4677)

ISBN-13: 978-0-595-37376-5 (pbk)
ISBN-13: 978-0-595-81773-3 (ebk)
ISBN-10: 0-595-37376-3 (pbk)
ISBN-10: 0-595-81773-4 (ebk)

Printed in the United States of America

Dedicated with love to

George and Diana Bruce
Steve and Martha Farmer
Randy and Rosa Jones
Mike and Carla Evans
Rex and Brenda Kennedy
Frank and Janie Bruce

Preface

This is Plan B.

Plan A was to write a weekly anecdote column titled "Wise Up!" for *The Athens News* in Athens, Ohio, then collect the anecdotes into books on various topics (Sports, Religion, Family, Good Deeds, Comedians, Music, Dance, Opera, Theater, Authors, Art, etc.), find a reputable literary agent, write bestseller after bestseller for a major publisher, and become rich and famous.

After finding out that Plan A was not working for me (I couldn't find a reputable agent), I had a choice:

1) Become cynical and bitter, and stop writing, or

2) Attempt to lead a life of wit and intelligence without fame and fortune, and write.

I have my moments of cynicism and bitterness (I follow politics to at least a limited extent); nevertheless, I have decided to continue to write and to attempt to lead a life of wit and intelligence. Thus, Plan B.

Plan B is to write a weekly anecdote column titled "Wise Up!" for *The Athens News* in Athens, Ohio, then collect the anecdotes into books on various topics (Sports, Religion, Family, Good Deeds, Comedians, Music, Dance, Opera, Theater, Authors, Art, etc.), and pay a Print-on-Demand company to print my books and list them on such Internet booksellers as amazon.com and barnesandnoble.com.

Both plans have their advantages and disadvantages. Plan A has the advantages of fame and fortune. Plan B avoids the disadvantages of fame and fortune. (Of course, I think that I could handle fame and fortune rather well, although they destroy some people.) Plan A has the disadvantages of my working hard to keep a reputable agent and major publishing company happy. Plan B has the advantages of my working hard to keep myself and a few dozen—or dare I say a few hundred—readers happy. Of course, with Plan A writing would be my profession, whereas with Plan B writing is my hobby.

I can't complain about following Plan B. iUniverse has been nothing but good to and for me. I read thousands of books I may not otherwise have read (I read the books, then retell—in my own words—a few good anecdotes from them), and I don't watch thousands of hours of television I might otherwise have watched.

Please enjoy this book, and if you wish, buy my other books. All anecdotes have been retold in my own words to avoid plagiarism.

250 Anecdotes About Religion

Animals

• Lawyers aren't always necessary to resolve disputes between neighbors. When country comedian Jerry Clower was growing up, some cows broke out of a neighbor's field one night, got into his stepfather's cornfield, and caused considerable damage. The next morning, Mr. Clower's stepfather went to the neighbor and said, "Your cows stayed in my field all night." The neighbor apologized: "I'm sorry. My cows broke through the fence. I didn't know they were in your field." The neighbor then said, "I tell you what let's do. Let's go get an impartial person living in the community, a member of our church, and ask him to walk over the field to determine the damage. Then he can tell me how much corn he believes those cows ate and I will put that much corn in your corncrib." That's exactly what they did. They agreed on a fair and honest man to serve as judge of the damage. He walked through the cornfield, then said, "Twenty bushels is what's due." Later that afternoon, the neighbor drove up and unloaded 20 bushels of corn into Mr. Clower's stepfather's corncrib.[1]

• In the summer of 1984, a small black dog began to come to the Catholic Church in Uvalde, Texas, where Msgr. Vincent Fecher serves. The dog arrived with its master, then stretched out on the lawn of the church. When the master left after Mass and went home, the dog stayed on the lawn, buried in the tall, cool grass, and it moved only to stay in the shade of a tree. At the end of the day, it went home until the following Sunday. Father Vincent says about the dog, "I always thought that its presence there, facing towards the sanctuary, was a silent sermon to everybody that even a dog had sense enough to come to church on Sundays."[2]

• Rabbi Stephen Wise met a man who boasted about a horse he had recently purchased. The horse could go as fast or as slow as you wanted. It could do any

---

1.   Source: Jerry Clower, *Life Everlaughter*, pp. 163-164.
2.   Source: Msgr. Vincent Fecher, *"The Lord and I": Vignettes from the Life of a Parish Priest*, p. 30.

work to which it was put. It was gentle, but it had spirit. It went when you wanted it to go, and it stopped when you wanted it to stop. It had no bad habits, plus it came immediately when called, and it didn't run off when confronted with something strange. Dr. Wise admired the horse, saying, "I wish that horse were a member of my congregation."[3]

• Buddhist texts say that animals should not be slaughtered for food, and Buddhist monks in Tibet make a vow not to kill any conscious being. While in his palace above the Tibetan capital city, Lhasa, the 14th Dalai Lama noticed people bringing in yaks for slaughter. By buying as many as he could, he saved 10,000 yaks from being slaughtered.[4]

Anti-Semitism

• During the Middle Ages, an anti-Semite falsely accused a Jew of killing a Christian, who had accidentally drowned in a well. However, the anti-Semite said that he would let God decide whether the Jew was guilty. He would write "guilty" on one slip of paper and "innocent" on a second slip and let the Jew choose one. Whichever slip of paper the Jew chose would determine whether he would go free. However, the Jew knew that the anti-Semite would write the word "guilty" on both slips of paper. Therefore, he chose a slip of paper, but he quickly put it in his mouth and swallowed it. "Look at the other slip of paper," he said. "That will tell you what the slip of paper I swallowed said."[5]

• Sherry Britton was a Jewish stripteaser. During World War II, an American soldier sent her a photograph of herself which he had taken from a dead Nazi soldier. Ms. Britton says, "If the German had known he was carrying around a picture of a Jewish girl, he wouldn't have had to be killed. He would have committed suicide."[6]

• Oscar Strauss was Jewish and rich—and happy to be both. Long ago, while vacationing in Lakewood, New Jersey, he saw a house that rented rooms. In front of the house was this sign: "No dogs or Jews allowed." A few minutes after he saw the sign, he bought the house and ordered the sign torn down.[7]

• Hadrian saw a Jew, who greeted him. Hadrian said, "Should a Jew see Hadrian and greet him? Cut off his head." Hadrian's soldiers carried off the Jew

3.   Source: Henry D. Spalding, *Jewish Laffs*, pp. 88-89.
4.   Source: Whitney Stewart, *The 14th Dalai Lama: Spiritual Leader of Tibet*, p. 54.
5.   Source: Rabbi Joseph Telushkin, *Jewish Humor*, pp. 150-151.
6.   Source: Tim Boxer, *The Jewish Celebrity Hall of Fame*, p. 270.
7.   Source: Joey Adams, *The Borscht Belt*, p. 144.

and beheaded him. Hadrian then saw a Jew, who did not greet him. Hadrian said, "Should a Jew see Hadrian and not greet him? Cut off his head."[8]

• Soviet Jews suffered from anti-Semitism. In one underground joke, several Communists go to Heaven, form a party cell, then discuss who should be the secretary. One of the Communists nominated God, but another Communist objected, "We can't elect Him! He had a son in Israel!"[9]

Baseball

• Sandy Koufax was a great Jewish major league pitcher. Umpire Tom Gorman was shocked to learn that Gene Oliver had hit .330 against Mr. Koufax, since Mr. Oliver was a left-handed hitter with a .220 batting average. He asked Mr. Oliver how he had managed to get so many hits against Mr. Koufax, and Mr. Oliver answered, "I'll tell you, but it's a secret. Don't tell anybody. He thinks I'm Jewish."[10]

• Tim Burke was both a New York Mets pitcher and a Born-Again Christian. In 1991, he was asked about Jesus and his career. He replied, "If Jesus were on the field, he'd be pitching inside and breaking up double plays."[11]

Censorship

• While Maury Maverick, Jr. was a member of the Texas House of Representatives in the 1950s, a bill came up advocating censorship in the Texas schools. Remarkably, an organization of Texas schoolteachers came out in support of the bill—after having been bought off with a pay raise. This scared Mr. Maverick, who was knowledgeable about bookburning by the Nazis and who wrote, "When that starts happening, that's the beginning of the end. That's when someone is going to start killing Jews, or Presbyterians, or Methodists, or conservatives, or liberals, or whatever. Somebody's going to get killed if that doesn't stop."[12]

• Nancy Garden is the lesbian author of *Annie on My Mind*, a young people's novel portraying lesbian characters in a positive manner. Religious groups in Kansas attacked the book, which was in school libraries, and a fundamentalist preacher even burned a copy of the book in public. However, students, parents,

---

8.   Source: Nahum N. Glatzer, editor, *Hammer on the Rock*, p. 107.
9.   Source: John Kolasky, collector and compiler, *Look, Comrade—The People are Laughing...*, p. 51.
10.   Source: Tom Gorman and Jerome Holtzman, *Three and Two!*, p. 77.
11.   Source: Michael J. Pellowski, *Baseball's Funniest People*, p. 85.
12.   Source: Maury Maverick, Jr., *Texas Iconoclast*, pp. 59-60.

and librarians protested when *Annie on My Mind* was removed from school libraries. One boy and his friends even checked approximately 3,000 books out of school district libraries to show how empty the shelves would be if controversial books were removed.[13]

• In the former USSR, members of the secret police attended church services to check the content of the sermons. Cardinal Wyszynski used to start his sermons by saying, "Brothers in Christ and delegates of the government...."[14]

Charity

• Rabbi Meir Shapiro of Lublin often said that he had learned from a beggar how to collect money for charity. A beggar had appeared at his door, and the good Rabbi had given him a generous handout, but the beggar asked for more. Someone present said that he was surprised that the beggar had asked for more money because the beggar had often accepted much smaller sums of money without arguing. The beggar replied that when he was given a small amount of money, it wasn't worth arguing about because what he would get if he won the argument? Another small amount of money. But a sizable amount of money was worth arguing about because if he won that argument he would get another sizable amount of money. Rabbi Meir Shapiro said, "Whenever I ask a donation from a wealthy man and he gives me a sizable sum, I tell that story."[15]

• Hei-zayemon was a wealthy philanthropist who tried to live his life in accordance with the insights gained by ancient sages. By using his money wisely, he relieved much of the hunger and misery of the poor people in his part of the world. One day, a monk showed up at his doorstep. Having heard of Hei-zayemon's philanthropy, the monk requested money to build a gate for his temple. Hearing this, Hei-zayemon laughed, saying, "I help people because I cannot bear to see them suffer. What's so bad about a temple without a gate?"[16]

• Entertainer Eddie Cantor put his knowledge of human nature to use while raising money for charity in what was reputed to be a tough town for fundraising. He did it by appearing to get sicker and sicker just before the fundraiser, even calling to see if someone could host the event for him at the last minute—which of course no one could. Because the people of the town thought Mr. Cantor was

13.   Source: Michael Thomas Ford, *Outspoken*, pp. 48-49, 64.
14.   Source: John Kolasky, collector and compiler, *Look, Comrade—The People are Laughing...*, p. 37.
15.   Source: Shmuel Himelstein, *A Touch of Wisdom, A Touch of Wit*, pp. 91-92.
16.   Source: Thomas Cleary, translator, *Zen Antics*, p. 1.

dying and was making his last request, he succeeded in raising $450,000 in a town where he normally would have been lucky to raise $150,000.[17]

• Andrew Carnegie was a very wealthy man who had a reputation for donating money to charitable causes. Mark Twain wrote him to say that he wanted to buy a $2 hymnbook, pointing out that "I will bless you, God will bless you and it will do a great deal of good." Mr. Twain then added a postscript: "Don't send the hymn-book—send me the two dollars."[18]

Children

• During a session of a junior church league, the preacher, Edwin Porter, was delayed, so he asked his oldest daughter, Janette, who was about 10 years old, to begin the session without him. The session started well, with 15 young children singing, "When the Roll is Called Up Yonder." Next came individual prayers, spoken out loud, during which Reverend Porter arrived in time to hear one young girl pray about his daughter Janette, "Dear Jesus, make that preacher's daughter quit stealing my sweetheart—and send him back to me." Another little girl prayed about one of Reverend Porter's young sons, "You know I need a husband—give me Edd Porter for my own." Yet another little girl—the daughter of two prominent members of his church—prayed, "Dear God, do keep Mama and Papa from fussing so much of the time."[19]

• Abraham, the first Jew, was the son of Terach, a maker of clay idols. When Abraham was a boy, he sometimes watched the shop while Terach was away. One day, while Terach was away from the shop, Abram (who was later called Abraham) broke all the idols. When Terach returned, he asked Abram what had happened. Abram said, "It was terrible. The smaller idols got angry and began fighting, then the bigger idols got angry and began fighting, and finally all the idols broke each other into bits." Terach said, "Idols don't get angry, and idols don't fight. They're made of clay—they just sit there." Abram replied, "So why do you worship them?"[20]

• A woman used to say "God!" whenever she was annoyed, which was several times a day, so her son—a regular attendant at Sunday School—decided to teach her a lesson. He called out, "Mommy!" She responded, but then he did not say anything. He did this five times in one day, and finally his mother said, "You

---

17. Source: Eddie Cantor, *Take My Life*, p. 261.
18. Source: Cyril Clemens, editor, *Mark Twain Anecdotes*, pp. 15-16.
19. Source: Alyene Porter, *Papa was a Preacher*, pp. 53-54.
20. Source: Jeffrey K. Salkin, *Being God's Partner*, pp. 145-146.

don't have anything to say, so why do you call me all the time?" Her son replied, "Mom, I called you five times, and already you have lost your patience. Each day, you call 'God!' more than five times. I wonder whether God has lost His patience with you."[21]

• Mrs. Miriam Pincus was a Rabbi's wife who used her histrionic ability to teach her young Hebrew School students Bible stories. While telling about David and Goliath, she used deep growls for the giant's voice and the voice of a hero for David. She also sang comic songs to keep her young students entertained. One Monday, three tots rang the Rabbi's doorbell. When the Rabbi came to the door, they asked, "Can Mrs. Pincus come out and play?"[22]

• Quaker unprogrammed meetings frequently include long periods of silence. A small child who was attending his first meeting sat quietly for a while, then he asked his mother, "Why are they all sitting so silently?" The mother hushed the child, but a Quaker rose and said, "Our first speaker this morning has put before us a most important question."[23]

• Mary Farwell's five-year-old son was playing with his Speak-and-Spell computer. He typed the word "G-O-D" into it, but was surprised when the computer told him, "Word not found." He tried it again, only to meet with the same unsatisfactory result. He then looked at his computer and said, "Jesus is not going to like this!"[24]

• A little boy had been naughty, so as punishment he was sent to bed after supper and was not allowed to watch his favorite TV program. His mother told him as he went to his room, "Pray to God so you can be a good boy tomorrow." "Why?" asked the little boy. "What's on TV tomorrow?"[25]

Christmas

• In Philadelphia, the Old First Reformed Church, United Church of Christ, always has a Christmas program in which a newborn baby from the congregation portrays the baby Jesus in a scene set in the manger. If a woman in the congregation gives birth to a girl, then Jesus is portrayed by a girl. If an African-American woman in the congregation gives birth, then Jesus is portrayed by an African-American baby. If a Hispanic woman in the congregation gives birth, then Jesus

---

21.   Source: Alexei D. Voskressenski, compiler and editor, *Cranks, Knaves, and Jokers of the Celestial*, p. 100.
22.   Source: Henry D. Spalding, *Jewish Laffs*, p. 34.
23.   Source: William H. Sessions, collector, *More Quaker Laughter*, pp. 49-50.
24.   Source: Edward K. Rowell, editor, *Humor for Preaching and Teaching*, p. 79.
25.   Source: Beulah Collins, collector, *For Benefit of Clergy*, p. 16.

is portrayed by a Hispanic baby. One year, a woman in the congregation gave birth to twins, so Jesus was portrayed by twins.[26]

• Comedian Lou Costello enjoyed trimming the Christmas tree by himself late on Christmas Eve after his children had gone to bed. One year, he arrived home very late on Christmas Eve because he had been detained at the radio station where *The Abbott and Costello Program* was produced, and he saw that the butler had decorated the tree. Mr. Costello was so disappointed that he went to his bedroom and cried.[27]

• A Sunday School class taught by Rolf E. Aaseng participated in a Christmas program which celebrated Jesus, the Light of the World. Four members of the class were supposed to carry large cardboard letters on stage to spell out the word STAR, but they got mixed up and displayed the letters in reverse order: RATS.[28]

• Michael Moore, the director of *Roger and Me*, went Christmas caroling in 1998 at the homes of the CEOs of the top tobacco companies. He took along with him the Awful Truth Choir, whose members have lost their voice boxes (aka larynxes) because they smoked.[29]

Church

• As a young pastor, William Woughter wanted to set new attendance records at his church. Therefore, he got hold of a number of old vinyl records and promised that whoever brought the most visitors to church on Sunday could publicly break a record over his head. Things went well for the first four Sundays—attendance was booming, and the records broke easily (pun definitely intended). On the fifth and final record-breaking Sunday, a young boy proudly led 27 visitors into the church. However, when the young boy took hold of the record and tried to break it over Pastor William's head, the record refused to break—despite the boy's several valiant attempts to break it. Later, a bruised Pastor William discovered that this particular record had been made with an unbreakable metal core.[30]

• The Second Ponce de Leon Baptist Church in Atlanta, Georgia, used to have a problem with parking. Nearby were two other places of worship: the Catholic Cathedral of Christ the King and the Episcopal Cathedral of St. Philip. Parking was hard to come by, and since these two churches met for worship earlier than

26. Source: Geneva M. Butz, *Christmas in All Seasons*, p. 42.
27. Source: Bob Thomas, *Bud & Lou*, p. 148.
28. Source: Rolf E. Aaseng, *Anyone Can Teach (they said)*, pp. 19-21.
29. Source: a December 1998 E-mail from Michael Moore to David Bruce (and several thousand other people).
30. Source: William Woughter, *All Preachers of Our God & King*, pp. 42-43.

the Second Ponce de Leon Baptist Church, the Catholics and Episcopalians used to park in the parking lot of the Baptist Church, resulting in a lack of parking spaces for the Baptists when they arrived for worship. Fortunately, the Second Ponce de Leon Baptist Church was able to solve the problem. Members of the Baptist Church simply put these bumper stickers on all the cars in its parking lot: "I'm Proud to Be a Southern Baptist."[31]

• Lots of people complain that churches don't have the facilities to compete with worldly entertainments, but country comedian Jerry Clower remembers offering to let his 14-year-old daughter Sue and one of her friends go with him on a trip to Hollywood, where they could meet celebrities Lorne Greene, David Janssen, Dinah Shore, and Mel Tillis. She told him, "Daddy, I love you and I'm so glad that you would arrange it to where me and one of my friends could go on this trip, but daddy, there's something going on at the church activities building I don't want to miss. I won't be able to go with you this time." When Mr. Clower heard his daughter say this, tears came to his eyes and he said, "Praise God from Whom all blessings flow."[32]

• A Vermonter was the only person to show up for early morning church services, so the minister asked the Vermonter what they should do. The Vermonter replied, "When I take a load of hay out into the field to feed the cows, and only one cow shows up, I don't turn her away hungry." Hearing this, the minister preached to his audience of one a sermon well over an hour long, then he asked the Vermonter what he thought of the sermon. The Vermonter replied, "When I take a load of hay out into the field to feed the cows, and only one cow shows up, I don't make her eat the whole load."[33]

• According to Quakers, speaking in unprogrammed meeting is not something that can be planned; instead, it is a matter of divine inspiration. John Warren attended a meeting in Maine, where people expected that he would speak. However, he didn't feel the Holy Spirit calling him to say anything, so he remained silent. After an hour in which no one spoke, the meeting was over, and Mr. Warren started walking out of the meetingplace. He overheard one boy tell another, "Didn't that beat the devil!" Mr. Warren turned around and told the boy, "That is what it is intended to do."[34]

• The Quakers, aka Friends, perform social (and religious) service as well as attend religious meetings. They often hold unprogrammed meetings in which

31. Source: Cal and Rose Samra, *Holy Hilarity*, pp. 17-18.
32. Source: Jerry Clower, *Let the Hammer Down!*, pp. 92-93.
33. Source: Rev. Francis J. Garvey, *Favorite Humor of Famous Americans*, p. 4.
34. Source: Irvin C. Poley and Ruth Verlenden Poley, *Friendly Anecdotes*, p. 37.

people are silent unless someone feels moved to speak. A person who knew nothing about Quakers attended a meeting and waited and waited for something to happen, but everyone remained silent. Finally, he nudged a Quaker and asked, "When does the service begin?" The Quaker replied, "The service begins when the meeting ends."[35]

• Mark Twain attended the church of his friend, the Reverend Joseph Twichell, and he became very interested in the sermon. After the church service was over, Mr. Twain told Reverend Twichell, "Joe, this mustn't happen again. When I go to church, I go for a good rest and quiet nap. Today I haven't been able to get a single wink. I tell you it won't do; and it must not happen again."[36]

• Ballerina Margot Fonteyn seldom attended church as a child, because her mother believed in letting children go to church only when they wanted. Why did Margot's mother believe that? Because when she was a little girl, she had been forced each Sunday to attend church three times. As a grownup, she went to church only for weddings.[37]

• A Sunday School teacher asked her class, "What do you think about when you see the church doors open to everyone who wants to worship God here?" An African-American student answered, "It's like walking into the heart of God."[38]

• After first arriving in Philadelphia, Benjamin Franklin attended a silent Quaker meeting. He fell asleep and did not wake until someone roused him when the meeting was over.[39]

Clothing

• Reb Simcha loved and admired his father, Reb Elchanan. When Reb Elchanan's shoes wore out, he gave his young son money to buy a new pair. When his son returned with the shoes, Reb Elchanan put them on and walked about. Seeing that his father looked perturbed, young Simcha asked what was wrong. Reb Elchanan replied, "My son, the laces upset me. I usually don't wear shoes with laces. Now I will have to spend time lacing my shoes, unlacing them when a lace breaks, tying them in the morning, untying them at night; they will require precious time that could be used instead for learning."[40]

---

35. Source: Chuck Fager, *Quakers are Funny!*, p. 78.
36. Source: Cyril Clemens, editor, *Mark Twain Anecdotes*, pp. 17-18.
37. Source: Margot Fonteyn, *Autobiography*, p. 19.
38. Source: Dick Van Dyke, *Faith, Hope, and Hilarity*, p. 95.
39. Source: Leila Merrell Foster, *Benjamin Franklin: Founding Father and Inventor*, p. 30.
40. Source: Rabbi Dovid Goldwasser, *It Happened in Heaven*, p. 172.

• A very stupid man had trouble getting dressed every morning because he could not find his clothes. One day, he had the idea of writing down where he put his clothes when he went to bed. The next morning, he looked at the writing, found his pants and put them on, then he looked at the writing again, found his shirt and put it on, and so on. But when he was dressed, he said, "But where am I? Where in the World am I?" He looked and looked, but he could not find where he was in the World. According to Rabbi Hanokh, we are like this man: We cannot find ourselves and we do not know where we are in the World.[41]

• Angelo Giuseppe Roncalli (who became Pope John XXIII) spent much time as Papal Nuncio in France, where he was often invited to dinners at which many women dressed fashionably but immodestly. Plans were made to ask the women to dress more modestly, but he rejected them, saying, "I have found that on such occasions it is not so much the woman at whom the crowd is looking but at me to see my reaction."[42]

Cold Weather

• In Rankin, Illinois, Al Karlstrom's father was the pastor of Grace Lutheran Church. Each Sunday morning, he would remind his children to shine their shoes in preparation for church. One very cold Sunday, his children were running late, so to save time shining their shoes, they used Vicks VapoRub instead of shoe polish. This worked out very well, as it made a nice shine. However, the steam radiators were running on high that Sunday to keep the cold out of the church, and the fumes coming off the pastor's children's shoes cleared up the heads of the congregation.[43]

• Rabbi Israel Salanter and two friends stayed at an inn in the midst of a very cold winter. He observed a serving girl drawing water and carrying the buckets in the cold, and when it came time for him and his friends to wash their hands before eating, he used very little water although his friends used lots of water. When asked about this, Rabbi Israel replied, "One should not be over strict in his observance of the law at the expense of someone else."[44]

41. Source: Martin Buber, *The Way of Man*, p. 30.
42. Source: Louis Michaels, *The Humor and Warmth of Pope John XXIII*, pp. 32-33.
43. Source: Cal and Rose Samra, *Holy Hilarity*, p. 13.
44. Source: Menahem G. Glenn, *Israel Salanter: Religious-Ethical Thinker*, p. 96.

Collections

• Art Linkletter's first public appearance was in church. His father was an evangelist whose income depended on the contributions the congregation made. Therefore, he would dress up his son in clean but patched clothing, then send him out to collect the offering while he told the congregation to "dig deep, brothers and sisters, for the good work."[45]

• Rabbi Stephen S. Wise took up a collection in his synagogue, and he told the worshippers, "Friends, tonight is the Sabbath when it is forbidden to carry money. Empty your pockets and put the money in the collection plates."[46]

Compassion

• Kamala Masters, who teaches Buddhist meditation, sailed with some friends in Hawaii. She felt seasick on the boat, so her friends urged her to get into the water. Because she didn't have a life vest, she didn't want to, but her friends persuaded her. She and some of her friends got in the water, a squall started blowing, and it blew the boat away from her. She started to panic, so her friends asked her to remember her Buddhist teachings, saying, "Kamala, what if these are your last moments? What do you want right now? Don't you want more love in your heart? Don't you want more compassion? What do you really want?" Kamala was very honest, and she admitted, "What I want right now is the boat!"[47]

• In the early 20th century, Rabbi Aryeh Levin was walking in a field with Rabbi Abraham Isaac Kook. When Rabbi Levin plucked a small flower from the field, Rabbi Kook started to tremble and told him that he refrained from plucking anything living unless some benefit could be gained from so doing, since every living thing, including plants, had a guardian angel looking out for it. From this experience, Rabbi Levin learned from Rabbi Kook to be compassionate toward all living things.[48]

Confession

• Songwriter Grant Clark brought a priest to see the great American scoundrel Wilson Mizner. Mr. Mizner told the priest, "Hello, Father. I went to confession

---

45. Source: Art Linkletter, *Kids Say the Darndest Things!*, p. 80.
46. Source: Philip Goodman, *Rejoice in Thy Festival*, pp. 34-35.
47. Source: Sharon Salzberg, *A Heart as Wide as the World*, pp. 166-167.
48. Source: Rabbi Joseph Telushkin, *Jewish Wisdom*, p. 440.

yesterday, and the priest left in the middle of it." Surprised, the priest asked, "Where did he go?" Mr. Mizner replied, "For the police."[49]

• A woman went to confession, but instead of saying, "Bless me, Father, for I have sinned," she absent-mindedly began to say a common table prayer: "Come, Lord Jesus, be our guest…." Fortunately, the priest had a sense of humor and asked, "What'd you do, bring your lunch?"[50]

Courage

• In Poland, Irene Gut Opdyke witnessed Nazis shooting unarmed Jews, and she prayed to God to ask Him "to give me responsibility, to bring me the opportunity to help, even if my own life should be taken." She helped many Jews, and she even hid several Jews at the villa of the elderly German major for whom she worked. (The architect of the villa had realized that war was coming, so he had built a hiding place under the gazebo. Much of the time the Jews were hidden there.) Unfortunately, the elderly German major discovered that she was hiding Jews. However, he said that he would protect her secret if she would become his mistress. She did. After the war, Ms. Opdyke said, "It was a small price to pay for the many lives."[51]

• At the trial by the Inquisition of Joan of Arc by biased judges who knew ahead of time that they would find her guilty no matter what defense she made, her judges asked her trick question after trick question. One example was this question: "Are you in God's grace?" If she answered that she was, her answer would be evidence that she was guilty of the sin of pride. If she answered that she was not, her answer would be evidence that God had rejected her. However, she was very intelligent—as well as justifiably defiant—and she answered, "If I am not, may God bring me to it; if I am, may God keep me in it."[52]

• Many people, including religious, resisted Nazi efforts to commit genocide against the Jews in Italy. Frequently, Jewish children were hidden in convents and monasteries. At a Carmine convent, unfortunately, Nazis discovered 50 Jewish children and took away most of them. Only two were saved—the mother superior succeeded in hiding two little girls under her skirts.[53]

---

49.   Source: Jim Tully, *A Dozen and One*, pp. 122-123.
50.   Source: Ken Alley, *Awkward Christian Soldiers*, pp. 90, 92.
51.   Source: Darryl Lyman, *Holocaust Rescuers: Ten Stories of Courage*, pp. 39, 42-43.
52.   Source: Don Nardo, *The Trial of Joan of Arc*, p. 50.
53.   Source: Victoria Sherrow, *The Righteous Gentiles*, p. 75.

• St. Athanasius tried to escape from some assassins by rowing a boat on a river. As he was rowing in one direction, the assassins approached him in a boat going in the other direction. When the assassins saw him, they cried out, "Where is the traitor Athanasius?" He avoided lying by answering, "Not far away," continued rowing, and escaped the assassins.[54]

Death

• According to Deuteronomy 6:5, "Thou shalt love the Lord thy God with all thy heart, and with all thy soul, and with all thy might." When Rabbi Akiba was about to be unjustly executed, it was the time of the Jewish prayer known as the Shema. (*Shema* is the first word of the Hebrew sentence which means "Hear, O Israel: The Lord our God, the Lord is One.") His disciples asked why he was reciting the Shema at this time. He replied that he had interpreted the verse "with all thy soul" to mean "even if He takes away your life" and he had always worried about when he could obey that commandment. Now that he had the opportunity of obeying the commandment, he would do so.[55]

• Entertainers were not always regarded with respect; long ago, they were regarded as wicked people who needed to repent. Jean-Baptiste Lully became very ill, and thinking he might die, he sent for a confessor. The priest told him, "In view of your stage-life, I want you to do penance by sacrificing something very dear to you." The priest then suggested that Lully allow him to throw into the fire the manuscript of a new opera that Lully had composed. Lully agreed, and the manuscript was burned. Instead of dying, Lully recovered. A friend remarked to him that it was a pity that the opera had been burned, but Lully told him, "Oh, that's all right. I have a copy of it."[56]

• A general swept through a region during wartime, creating havoc and terror wherever he went. He entered a temple and was surprised that the Zen master was not terrified of him. The general asked the Zen master, "Don't you know that I can run this sword through your body without batting an eye?" The Zen master replied, "Don't you know that I can have a sword run through my body without batting an eye?" The general bowed to the Zen master, then left him in peace.[57]

---

54. Source: Anthony Weston, *A Practical Companion to Ethics*, p. 30.
55. Source: William B. Silverman, *Rabbinic Wisdom and Jewish Values*, p. 30.
56. Source: Henry T. Finck, *Musical Laughs*, p. 289.
57. Source: Jack Kornfield and Christina Feldman, *Soul Food*, p. 43.

• Martin Luther King's mother, like himself, died because of violence. On June 30, 1974, while playing the organ in church, she was shot and killed, as was a church deacon. The murderer was Marcus Wayne Chenault, a mentally disturbed African American who said he had killed them because they were Christians. He was tried, found guilty, and sentenced to die. However, the King family opposed the death penalty, and the sentence was later reduced to life in prison.[58]

• Marpa was a great Tibetan teacher, who as a Buddhist taught that everything is an illusion. Unfortunately, his oldest son died and Marpa grieved greatly. A Buddhist monk came to him and said, "I don't understand. You teach us that everything is an illusion. Yet you are crying. If everything is an illusion, then why do you grieve so deeply?" Marpa replied, "Indeed, everything is an illusion. And the death of a child is the greatest of these illusions."[59]

• A man dying of AIDS told his nurse that he would like to become a Catholic. Immediately, the nurse telephoned her priest and asked him to come right over. However, upon hearing that the man was dying of AIDS, the priest hesitated, saying that this was a controversial situation. The nurse responded, "This man is dying, and he will not live much longer. Get your butt over here now, or I'll baptize him myself." The priest came right over.[60]

• When Wilson Mizner lay dying after a life devoted to gambling, illegal activities, and the spending of money, a clergyman who was very successful in obtaining the deathbed conversions of rascals was brought in to him. Mr. Wilson declined to be converted, saying, "I don't expect too much. You can't be a rascal for 40 years and then cop a plea the last minute. God keeps better books than that." A few minutes later, he died.[61]

• In 1949, Mother Teresa found a dying man lying on a sidewalk in Calcutta. She asked a nearby hospital if she could bring the man in, but she was not allowed to. Therefore, she visited a pharmacist to get medicine for the man, but by the time she returned, the man had died. Mother Teresa had witnessed such callousness more than once. She said, "They look after a dog or a cat better than a fellow man."[62]

58. Source: Michael A. Schuman, *Martin Luther King: Leader for Civil Rights*, pp. 107-108.
59. Source: Jack Kornfield and Christina Feldman, *Soul Food*, p. 233.
60. Source: Tim Unsworth, *Here Comes Everybody!*, p. xii.
61. Source: John Burke, *Rogue's Progress: The Fabulous Adventures of Wilson Mizner*, p. 278.
62. Source: Anne Schraff, *Women of Peace: Nobel Peace Prize Winners*, p. 59.

• Early American colonists suffered from high rates of infant mortality. Often, a family would keep giving their children the same Christian name until one child finally survived. In addition, women frequently died in childbirth. At some old cemeteries, the husband would be buried along with several of his wives and several of their children who had died as infants or in childhood.[63]

• When Pope Pius II died, Dr. Arthur Schlesinger, Jr., announced the death to his Harvard class titled "Intellectual History of America from 1776 to the Present." He stated that because he had read it in the *Christian Science Monitor* he knew it was true, and he added, "I anxiously await my copy when Mary Baker Eddy decides to come back to life."[64]

• Bodhidharma, a Buddhist monk, founded both Zen Buddhism and early karate after traveling from India to China. According to legend, after Bodhidharma died in China, he was seen walking back to India while wearing one sandal. To check on the story, Bodhidharma's coffin was opened—nothing was in it, except one sandal.[65]

• "Shoeless Joe" Jackson was kicked out of professional baseball after being suspected of helping the Chicago Black Sox throw the 1919 World Series—despite batting .375 in the series. When he died, his last words were, "I'm going to meet the Greatest Umpire of all, now. I know that He will judge me innocent."[66]

• When Zen master Tekisui was on his deathbed, another Zen master named Keichu came by his house. He left a box of cakes for Tekisui, and he also gave this message to a servant to give to Tekisui: "You're old enough to die without regret." When Tekisui heard the message, he smiled.[67]

• Franz Liszt was buried at Bayreuth, where he had died, although some people wanted his body to be moved and buried at Weimar. However, Liszt was of the Order of Franciscans, whose rules specify that members of the order must be buried where they die.[68]

---

63. Source: Helen Chappell, *The Chesapeake Book of the Dead*, pp. 27, 31.
64. Source: a May 11, 1998 personal letter to David Bruce by a person who wishes to remain anonymous.
65. Source: Luana Metil and Jace Townsend, *The Story of Karate: From Buddhism to Bruce Lee*, p. 17.
66. Source: Joe Thompson, *Growing Up with "Shoeless Joe,"* p. 125.
67. Source: Lucien Stryk and Takashi Ikemoto, selectors and translators, *Zen: Poems, Prayers, Sermons, Anecdotes, Interviews*, p. 120.
68. Source: Henry T. Finck, *Musical Laughs*, p. 174.

• Comedy writer Barney Dean refused to take hospitals seriously. On his way to the hospital where he would die, he told a friend, "You'd better take my wallet. I don't want these nuns rolling me."[69]

• Rabbi Stephen S. Wise tells us that when a man named Freeman (alas, he doesn't give a first name) died, he requested that this epitaph be carved on his tombstone: "He died learning."[70]

Easter

• On Easter, worshippers at McMasters United Methodist Church in Turtle Creek, Pennsylvania, saw two large red letters—M and T—behind the altar. Of course, the letters stood for the good news about Jesus' tomb—that it was eMpTy. The pastor, Reverend Jeffrey D. Sterling, wanted to quiz the children about the meaning of the letters during the children's lesson, so after all the children had gathered at the front of the church, he asked them, "What's different about the church today, kids?" His own daughter answered the question. Ignoring the large red letters, she said, "It's full, Dad!"[71]

• Country comedian Jerry Clower is a devout Christian who attends Baptist church each Sunday, and sometimes he gets a little upset at Christians who attend church only on Easter. One year, while driving to Easter services, he told his wife, Homerline, "Darling, if there's a lost man sitting in the pew where I usually sit this morning, on Easter Sunday, I'll kneel by him and pray or stand outside in the rain. He can have my seat. But if a Baptist is in my seat that ain't been there since last Easter, he's getting *up*."[72]

Education

• When the scholar Rabbi Bun died at an early age, Rabbi Zera spoke highly of his scholarly labors, comparing him to a worker in a king's vineyard who worked hard for two or three hours. The king called the worker to him, and they walked together. At the end of the day, the king paid all his laborers, including the man who had worked for only a few hours, the same wage. The other workers complained, saying that they had worked for the entire day, and they asked, "Is it right that he should receive the same wages we do?" The king responded, "Why are you angry? This man has done as much work in two or three hours as the rest

---

69.   Source: Bob Hope, *The Road to Hollywood*, p. 41.
70.   Source: Stephen S. Wise, *How to Face Life*, p. 59.
71.   Source: Cal and Rose Samra, *Holy Humor*, p. 60.
72.   Source: Jerry Clower, *Let the Hammer Down!*, p. 63.

of you have done in a whole day." And so, Rabbi Zera said, "Thus, too, Rabbi Bun has accomplished more in the realm of the Torah during his 28 years than a diligent student could ordinarily accomplish in 100 years."[73]

• A university professor visited Japanese Zen master Nan-in. The professor was supposed to be there to learn about Zen from Nan-in, but it quickly became apparent from the professor's comments that he believed that he was already an expert in Zen. Therefore, when Nan-in served the professor tea, he filled the professor's teacup full and then continued pouring so that the tea ran to the ground. The professor cried out, "Stop! It is already full! No more will go in!" Nan-in replied, "Like this cup, you are full of your own opinions. How can I show you Zen unless you first empty your cup?"[74]

• A Buddhist teacher from India visited the United States. When he was asked what he thought of Buddhist practices in America, he said that they reminded him of a person in a rowboat rowing and rowing, yet getting nowhere because the rowboat is tied to the dock. Many people in the United States devote much time and effort to meditation about lovingkindness, he said, but they forget to practice lovingkindness toward other people in the course of their daily activities.[75]

• Peter Cartwright was a pioneer circuit-riding preacher who was suspicious of educated preachers. He met an educated preacher who addressed him in Greek in order to humiliate him. Not to be outdone, Mr. Cartwright spoke to him in German. The educated preacher, who did not know Hebrew, concluded that Mr. Cartwright had replied to him in that language, and he said that Mr. Cartwright was the first educated Methodist preacher that he had ever seen.[76]

• Governor Wang questioned the teaching methods of Zen master Rinzai. Governor Wang asked if the monks read sutras. Rinzai said they did not. Governor Wang asked if the monks learned meditation. Rinzai said they did not. Governor Wang then asked, "If they don't read sutras or learn meditation, what are on earth are they doing here?" Rinzai replied, "All I do is make them become Buddhas and Bodhisattvas."[77]

• Not being able to spell may have advantages. A young Quaker woman attending Oxford University was very intelligent but completely unable to spell. On a visit to the continent, she filled out a form in Customs. In the space by the

73. Source: Jakob J. Petuchowski, translator and editor, *Our Masters Taught*, pp. 29-30.
74. Source: Paul Reps, *Zen Flesh, Zen Bones*, p. 19.
75. Source: Sharon Salzberg, *Lovingkindness*, p. 171.
76. Source: J. Vernon Jacobs, compiler, *450 True Stories from Church History*, p. 95.
77. Source: Perle Besserman and Manfred Steger, *Crazy Clouds*, p. 43.

word "Occupation," she wrote, "Nun"—and she was amazed at how much quicker than her traveling companions she passed through Customs.[78]

• When Rolf E. Aaseng first began teaching Sunday School, he and another teacher complained about the rooms they taught in. Mr. Aaseng taught in a stinky basement, and the other teacher taught in the kitchen. However, yet another teacher topped them both—because of lack of space, she was forced to teach her Sunday School class in the women's restroom![79]

• Rabbi Stephen S. Wise knew a couple who had gotten their son accepted into an excellent boys' school before their son was even born. Rabbi Wise asked what they would have done if they had had a girl, but they assured him that they had considered that and had also applied for their child's admission into an excellent girls' school.[80]

• Rabbi Jacob Joseph grew up in a very poor household in Lithuania. His father, who worked in a brewery, used to scrimp on food so that he could pay his son's tuition. Because of this experience, Rabbi Joseph knew that often poor people value Jewish education more than rich people.[81]

• A school in Germany had only one Jewish student. The teacher told her, "Just like all the Jews, you are greedy. Your father pays tuition for only one student, but you are learning enough for three."[82]

Enlightenment

• A student came to Zen master Suiwo, seeking enlightenment, so Suiwo gave him a problem to solve: "Hear the sound of one hand." The student meditated for three years, but he never solved the problem and so did not achieve enlightenment. Finally, the student asked to return home in disgrace because he had not become enlightened. Suiwo urged the student to stay another week, which the student did, but without becoming enlightened. Suiwo again urged the student to stay another week, then five days, which the student did, but always with the same lack of results. Finally, Suiwo told the student, "Meditate for three days longer, then if you fail to attain enlightenment, you had better kill yourself." The student attained enlightenment.[83]

78. Source: William H. Sessions, collector, *Laughter in Quaker Grey*, p. 57.
79. Source: Rolf E. Aaseng, *Anyone Can Teach (they said)*, pp. 13-15.
80. Source: Stephen S. Wise, *How to Face Life*, pp. 16-17.
81. Source: Menahem G. Glenn, *Israel Salanter: Religious-Ethical Thinker*, p. 91.
82. Source: Harvey Mindess, *The Chosen People?*, p. 34.
83. Source: Paul Reps, *Zen Flesh, Zen Bones*, p. 45.

• Zen master Ikkyu accepted an invitation to become the abbot of a subtemple; however, at a banquet held after he became abbot, several wealthy people told him that in return for their making large donations to the subtemple, they expected him to give them *inka*—written confirmation that they had become enlightened. Refusing to be bribed, Ikkyu and his chief disciples immediately left the subtemple.[84]

Etiquette

• Rumi, the founder of the Whirling Dervishes, understood and practiced good etiquette. When an Armenian butcher bowed to him seven times, Rumi returned the bows. On another occasion, several children in a group bowed to him, and Rumi bowed to each of the children. One child was far off, and he called to Rumi, "Wait for me until I come." Rumi waited, the child arrived and bowed to him, and Rumi returned the child's bow.[85]

• In Philadelphia, a homeless person named Carlos was very hungry and wondering where his next meal would come from. A priest appeared and gave him a sandwich. Carlos was so hungry that he ate the sandwich before remembering to thank the priest. After eating the sandwich, he looked for the priest, but the priest had disappeared. After that, Carlos always thanked someone who gave him food, then he ate the food.[86]

Faith

• R' Shimon Sofer of Cracow was very young when a heretic asked him a question that he could not answer, so he approached his father, the Chasam Sofer, and asked for the answer to the question. The Chasam Sofer did not answer the question right away, but waited a few days, then easily answered the question. When his son asked why he had waited, although he could have answered the question right away, the Chasam Sofer replied, "I wanted to teach you that in questions of faith, one does not have to worry if he does not have an immediate answer. If he doesn't have an answer today, he will have it tomorrow. Meanwhile, there is no reason to lose faith."[87]

• Sheikh Abu al-Bistami had several disciples who complained that the Devil had taken away their faith. After hearing this, the Sheikh summoned the Devil

---

84. Source: Perle Besserman and Manfred Steger, *Crazy Clouds*, p. 74.
85. Source: Shams al-Din Ahmad Aflaki, *Legends of the Sufis*, p. 51.
86. Source: Geneva M. Butz, *Christmas in All Seasons*, p. 5.
87. Source: Shmuel Himelstein, *A Touch of Wisdom, A Touch of Wit*, p. 57.

and asked if his disciples' complaint was true. The Devil told him, "I never force anyone to give up their faith because I fear God too much to do that. However, many people foolishly throw away their faith for trivial reasons. Whenever that happens, I take the faith they have thrown away."[88]

• A young man who doubted the existence of God asked Menachem Mendel, Rabbi of Kotzker, where God really lived. The Rabbi answered, "Wherever He is admitted."[89]

Family

• Catholic priests may not have biological children of their own, but they do have families. An American, Msgr. Vincent Fecher had been studying in Rome for five years, but then he was assigned to be the priest at a Catholic church in the small town of Uvalde, Texas. He was walking with an Italian friend and discussing his return to America when the Italian friend said, "I guess it's only natural that you should want to go back to America and be near your family." Father Vincent said, with conviction, "My family is right here!" Then he continued, more quietly, "Gino, you're my family. I am closer to all of you here than I am to my own brothers and sisters, some of whom I have not seen in 15 years. Some of whom I hardly know." Since saying that, Father Vincent has become even more convinced that the "parish is my real family."[90]

• Dr. Stephen S. Wise was introduced in an African-American church by a minister who said, "I have the honor to introduce you to a man who is conceited to be America's greatest orator." When Dr. Wise related this story to his family later, they commented, "How well this minister knows you."[91]

Food

• Do you know the first drink and food to be drunk and eaten on the moon? According to astronaut Buzz Aldrin, "The very first liquid ever poured on the moon and the first food eaten there, were communion elements." While Mike Collins orbited the moon, and Buzz Aldrin and Neil Armstrong were on the moon in the *Eagle*, Mr. Aldrin requested a few minutes of silence from Houston. Mr. Aldrin then opened some plastic packages containing the communion wine

88.   Source: James Fadiman and Robert Frager, *Essential Sufism*, p. 172.
89.   Source: S. Felix Mendelsohn, *Here's a Good One*, p. 157.
90.   Source: Msgr. Vincent Fecher, *"The Lord and I": Vignettes from the Life of a Parish Priest*, pp. 123-124.
91.   Source: S. Felix Mendelsohn, *Here's a Good One*, p. 179.

and bread and poured the wine into a chalice his church had given to him. After Mr. Aldrin had read the words, "I am the vine—you are the branches. Whoever remains in Me, and I in him, will bear much fruit; for you can do nothing without Me," he and Mr. Armstrong took communion.[92]

• While the Israelites were wandering in the desert, they decided to ask God to dinner. Their leader, Moses, explained that God is not a physical being and so He does not eat. But when Moses went up on the mountain to talk with God, God said to him that He would accept the Israelites' dinner invitation. All the next day, the Israelites prepared dinner for God. An old man, poor and hungry, arrived and asked for something to eat, but the Israelites were too busy to give the old man some food. That evening, the Israelites looked for God, but they didn't see Him. The next morning Moses went up on the mountain and asked God why He had not come for the dinner. God replied, "I did come. If you had fed the old man, you would have fed Me."[93]

• Back in the days when Catholics did not eat meat on Friday, Rear Admiral George Dufek and Father Linehan (a geo-physicist from Boston College), were at the South Pole. Rear Admiral Dufek pulled some sandwiches out for lunch, but Father Linehan looked at the sandwiches, saw that they were made with ham and roast beef, and said, "None for me. It's Friday, you know." Rear Admiral Dufek replied, "If you'll step about 15 paces to the left, it will still be Thursday." Father Linehan did so, then he enjoyed lunch.[94]

• Some of the food eaten on the Jewish Sabbath is especially good. For example, the bread known as Hallah is eaten on the Sabbath. Once a Jew had a visitor who ate only the expensive Hallah but did not touch the common, inexpensive bread. The host hinted to the visitor, "Taste the bread," but the visitor continued to eat the Hallah, remarking that Hallah is better than plain bread. "True," said the host, "but it's expensive." The guest replied, "The extra expense is worth it."[95]

• While walking along a river, two monks noticed a lettuce leaf floating downstream. "How sad," said one of the monks, who knew that Zen master Gizan lived one mile upstream. "Gizan has started to waste food." Just then, Gizan burst out of the bushes, panting and sweating, jumped into the river, and began to swim downstream after the lettuce leaf. The two monks bowed low in the direction of Zen master Gizan, then they continued their walk.[96]

---

92.   Source: Joey Adams, *The God Bit*, pp. 303-304.
93.   Source: James Fadiman and Robert Frager, *Essential Sufism*, pp. 11-12, 221.
94.   Source: Hiley H. Ward, editor, *Ecumania*, p. 59.
95.   Source: Philip Goodman, *Rejoice in Thy Festival*, p. 28.

• A rich man came to the Maggid of Mezeritch and tried to impress him with his piety. When the Maggid asked the rich man what he ate, he replied that he ate nothing but bread. The Maggid shook his head sadly, then he ordered him to eat cake. When the rich man asked why, the Maggid explained, "If you are content to eat bread, you will believe that the poor can live by eating stones, but if you eat cake, you will give bread to the poor."[97]

• On the American frontier, getting enough food to eat was sometimes a major struggle and thus took precedence over other things. One frontier preacher was giving a sermon when some dogs near the camp started barking at a bear. The preacher listened for a moment, then told the women to pray while he and the other men took off after the bear. After they had killed the bear, the preacher resumed his sermon.[98]

• Zen master Taji was on his deathbed. His disciples knew that he liked a certain kind of cake, so they went from shop to shop in Tokyo until they found the kind of cake he liked, then they brought him a piece. After Taji had eaten the cake, his disciples asked if he had any last words for them. "Yes," he replied, and as his disciples leaned toward him, he said, "My, but this cake is delicious." Then he died.[99]

• The Buddhists believe in a realm of being that is populated by "hungry ghosts." They have enormous bodies but very small mouths, so they are constantly feeding themselves to fill up the emptiness inside. Thich Nhat Hanh, a Buddhist teacher in Vietnam, was asked what the realm of the hungry ghosts is like. He replied, "America."[100]

• A preacher ate a couple of Sunday dinners with the same farming family, who served chicken each time. After the second dinner, the preacher remarked on a hen which he said was particularly proud looking. "She should be proud," said the farmer. "She has two children in the ministry."[101]

• After Mother Teresa gave a piece of bread to a small, hungry girl lost in the streets, the girl began to eat the bread very slowly, crumb by crumb. Mother Teresa said, "Eat, eat the bread! Aren't you hungry!" The girl replied, "I am just afraid that when I run out of bread, I'll still be hungry."[102]

96. Source: Lucien Stryk and Takashi Ikemoto, selectors and translators, *Zen: Poems, Prayers, Sermons, Anecdotes, Interviews*, p. xlii.

97. Source: Elie Wiesel, *Souls on Fire*, pp. 72-73.

98. Source: Ross Phares, *Bible in Pocket, Gun in Hand*, p. 26.

99. Source: Sushila Blackman, compiler and editor, *Graceful Exits*, p. 28.

100. Source: Sharon Salzberg, *Lovingkindness*, p. 161.

101. Source: Ivy Moody, *Illustrations with a Point*, p. 12.

• God cares more about how you earn your money than what you eat. As Israeli economist Meir Tamari has pointed out, in the Torah, over 100 commandments concern economics, but only 24 commandments make up the foundation for traditional Jewish dietary practice.[103]

• A starving dervish asked a rich man for food, but the rich man asked him to return the next day, when he was holding a feast. The dervish replied, "Give me some food today, so that I may live until tomorrow to attend your feast."[104]

Freedom of Religion

• The Puritans faced religious discrimination in Great Britain, so they moved to Massachusetts Bay—where they engaged in discrimination. When the Quakers arrived in Massachusetts Bay in 1655, the Puritans whipped them, put them in prison, then banished them. After some Quakers returned to Massachusetts Bay, the Puritans passed a law calling for the execution by hanging of any Quaker who had been banished, but returned. The Puritans also banned Catholic priests and sometimes whipped and imprisoned Baptists. James Madison put freedom of religion into the Bill of Rights in order to outlaw such religious discrimination.[105]

• The Puritans did not practice freedom of religion. When Native Americans in New England did not keep the Sabbath, the Puritans used that as an excuse to seize their lands.[106]

Gays and Lesbians

• Not all churches are loving. A minister speculated that the son of a family in the church was gay, and he started spreading that speculation around. The speculation turned out to be true. Very quickly, the family of the gay boy came under verbal attack from other members of the church. Meanwhile, the gay boy was being both verbally and physically attacked at school. The mother of the family complained about the church: "Instead of being overwhelmed by love, we were overwhelmed by judgment." The family was unwilling to give up on religion

---

102. Source: José Luis González-Balado, compiler, *Mother Teresa: In My Own Words*, p. 84.
103. Source: Jeffrey K. Salkin, *Being God's Partner*, p. 113.
104. Source: Massud Farzan, *Another Way of Laughter*, p. 50.
105. Source: J. Edward Evans, *Freedom of Religion*, p. 17.
106. Source: Anita Louise McCormick, *Native Americans and the Reservation in American History*, p. 27.

because of a few bigots, including a bigoted minister, so the family left that church and attended a much more loving Episcopal church.[107]

• Gays and lesbians have their own church in which to worship God. The worldwide network of Metropolitan Community Churches is nondenominational. In addition, many gay and lesbian groups exist within established denominations. Integrity is a group for gay and lesbian Episcopalians, Dignity is for gay and lesbian Catholics, and Affirmation is the name of two groups, one for gay and lesbian Mormons and one for gay and lesbian United Methodists. Some synagogues specifically serve gay, lesbian, and bisexual Jews—the oldest such synagogue is Temple Beth Chayim Chadashim in Los Angeles whose Rabbi, Lisa Edwards, is a lesbian.[108]

• As a lesbian, Lois Hoxie didn't feel comfortable at a Catholic Church in the Oakland, California, area, so she stopped attending. Shortly afterward, she was surprised when the priest stopped by to visit her and asked, "Why don't you go to church?" She replied, "I don't feel welcome at Saint Pascal's." "Why is that?" the priest asked. She replied, "Because I'm gay." The priest asked, "Yes, but why don't you feel welcome at Saint Pascal's?" The priest didn't mind that she was gay; however, other Catholics made her feel unwelcome, so eventually she became a Friend, aka Quaker.[109]

• Following a Gay Pride march, several gay men and lesbians gathered at a church for worship. Unfortunately, some protesters arrived and shouted, "Sinners! Repent of your sick and evil ways!" The gay men, lesbians, and the minister of the church began chanting in return, "Jesus loves me and Jesus loves you. Jesus loves me and Jesus loves you." This angered the protesters, and they shouted, "Jesus hates you! Jesus hates you!" In this case, the protesters won—they shouted down the gay men, the lesbians, the minister, and the message, "Jesus loves me and Jesus loves you."[110]

• Lesbian comedian Kate Clinton appeared on a daytime talk show, the producers of which decided to create controversy by busing in a group of churchwomen to sit in the audience and watch the show. To the surprise of the producers, the churchwomen fully supported the rights of gays and lesbians.[111]

• When people tell lesbian comedian Judy Carter that homosexuality is a sin against God, she replies, "So is judging people."[112]

107. Source: Chastity Bono, *Family Outing*, pp. 232-233.
108. Source: Michael Thomas Ford, *Outspoken*, pp. 143-144, 161.
109. Source: Zsa Zsa Gershick, *Gay Old Girls*, pp. 227-228.
110. Source: Gerald Fuller, *Stories for All Seasons*, pp. 131-132.
111. Source: Kate Clinton, *Don't Get Me Started*, pp. 120-121.

Heaven and Hell

• Among Mark Twain's favorites of the books he had written was *Personal Recollections of Joan of Arc*, about a French heroine for whom Mr. Twain had enormous respect. Mr. Twain met the Archbishop of Orléans, who told him that St. Joan (aka the Maid of Orléans) would no doubt see to it that anyone who wrote so beautifully about her would get into Heaven. Mr. Twain replied that he would be "perfectly satisfied" in the next life if he were near Joan of Arc and as far away as possible from her enemies.[113]

• Mark Twain attended a large dinner where the topic of conversation was Heaven and Hell. Mr. Twain remained quiet—something very uncharacteristic of him. When a woman asked him, "Why don't you say something? I would like to hear your opinion," he replied, "Madam, you must excuse me. I am silent of necessity—I have friends in both places!"[114]

• A Cardinal and a Congressman died and went to Heaven. The Cardinal was given barely adequate accommodations, but the Congressman was given a luxurious mansion to live in. The Cardinal asked St. Peter about the different accommodations, and St. Peter replied, "In Heaven we have lots of Cardinals—but he's our only Congressman."[115]

• Will Rogers was a human being who felt for other human beings. When fellow comedian Eddie Cantor was sad because his grandmother wasn't still alive when he was a hit in the 1917 Ziegfeld Follies, Will comforted him by saying, "Now, Eddie, what makes you think she didn't see you? And from a very good seat?"[116]

• A man asked a Zen master what would happen after the Zen master died. The Zen master calmly replied, "I will enter Hell." "Enter Hell?" the man said. "You are a paragon of virtue. Why would you enter Hell?" The Zen master answered, "If I don't enter Hell, who will enlighten you?"[117]

• Radio announcers always keep a record handy to play in case a live feed goes dead. When technical difficulties interrupted a Sunday morning sermon broad-

---

112. Source: Judy Carter, *The Homo Handbook*, p. 132.
113. Source: Cyril Clemens, "Mark Twain's Religion," p. 13.
114. Source: Dick Van Dyke, *Faith, Hope, and Hilarity*, p. 94.
115. Source: Rev. Francis J. Garvey, *Favorite Humor of Famous Americans*, p. 9.
116. Source: Eddie Cantor, *Take My Life*, p. 106.
117. Source: Chih-Chung Tsai (editor and illustrator) and Kok Kok Kiang (translator), *The Book of Zen*, p. 25.

cast, the announcer grabbed the handy record and played it. It was Cab Calloway singing, "You'll Never Get to Heaven That Way."[118]

• Agnellus Andrew used to act as a consultant on Catholic affairs for the BBC. BBC TV producer Hugh Burnett asked him how he could get the official Catholic view concerning Heaven and Hell. Mr. Andrew sent him a one-word memo: "Die."[119]

Holocaust

• In southeast Poland, Andrew Sheptitsky was head of the Greek Catholic Church. During World War II, he helped save over 150 Jews from the Nazis by hiding them in monasteries, convents, churches, and his home. To a Jewish man who had been hidden in a monastery, and who sometimes pretended to be a monk in order to avoid capture by the Nazis, Mr. Sheptitsky said, "I want you to be a good Jew, and I am not saving you for your own sake. I am saving you for your people. I do not expect any reward, nor do I expect you to accept my faith."[120]

• Archbishop Angelo Giuseppe Roncalli, later to be Pope John XXIII, was apostolate delegate to Turkey during the days of the Nazis. The German ambassador, Franz von Papen, came to him to see if Rome would support the German army's fight against the "atheistic Communists." Archbishop Roncalli was unimpressed and replied, "What shall I tell them about the millions of Jews your countrymen are murdering in Germany and in Poland?"[121]

• During World War II, Father Jonas of Vidukle, Lithuania, used his church to hide 30 Jewish children. The Nazis discovered that Jewish children were hiding there, and they battered down the door of the church and entered. Father Jonas told the Nazis that they would have to kill him before they could harm the children. The Nazis murdered Father Jonas, then they murdered the children.[122]

• Movie director Steven Spielberg is Jewish, and some of his relatives survived being in concentration camps during the Holocaust. As a three-year-old boy, he learned to count by reading the numbers tattooed on a relative's forearm.[123]

---

118. Source: Glenhall Taylor, *Before Television*, p. 22.
119. Source: John Deedy, *A Book of Catholic Anecdotes*, p. 11.
120. Source: Darryl Lyman, *Holocaust Rescuers: Ten Stories of Courage*, pp. 75, 81.
121. Source: Louis Michaels, *The Humor and Warmth of Pope John XXIII*, p. 53.
122. Source: Victoria Sherrow, *The Righteous Gentiles*, p. 43.
123. Source: Tom Powers, *Steven Spielberg: Master Storyteller*, p. 20.

Humility

• The Dalai Lama gave a series of lectures in Tucson, Arizona. Although his English is good, he lectured in Tibetan about Shantideva's *Guide to the Bodhisattva's Way of Life,* and a translator spoke in English. At one point, the Dalai Lama told the translator, "You're mistaken. That's not what I said." They then argued about a sentence by Shantideva—the Dalai Lama thought the sentence was "She said that to him," but the translator thought the sentence was "He said that to her." After discussing the sentence for a while, the Dalai Lama looked the sentence up, then he started laughing and admitted, "Oh, I made a mistake." Although he was lecturing in front of 1,200 people, he freely admitted that the mistake was his.[124]

• One day Pope John XXIII went to a nursing home that was run by nuns so he could visit a dying prelate. The nun who answered the door was understandably astonished to see the Pope, and she almost fainted. However, the Pope told her, "No need to be alarmed, Sister. After all, I'm only the Pope."[125]

Husbands and Wives

• The private Groucho (real name: Julius) was as funny as the public Groucho. His first wedding was like a scene out of a Marx Brothers movie. Harpo hid behind a potted plant and made it appear to be walking around the room. When the minister said, "We are gathered here in holy matrimony," Groucho's response was, "It may be holy to you, Reverend, but we have other ideas." And when the minister asked, "Do you, Julius, take this woman to be your lawful wedded wife," Groucho replied, "Well, we've gone this far. We might as well go through with it."[126]

• A young, newlywed Hindu couple came to Mother Teresa and gave her much money, which they had saved by not celebrating their wedding, not buying wedding clothes, and not going on a honeymoon. When Mother Teresa asked why they had made such a sacrifice, they answered, "We love each other so much that we wanted to share the joy of our love with those you serve."[127]

• An atheist heckled Billy Sunday during a sermon by interrupting with questions designed to embarrass believers. For example, the heckler asked, "Who was

---

124. Source: Sharon Salzberg, *A Heart as Wide as the World,* pp. 142-143.

125. Source: Henri Fesquet, collector, *Wit and Wisdom of Good Pope John,* p. 35.

126. Source: Arthur Marx, *Life With Groucho,* p. 54.

127. Source: José Luis González-Balado, compiler, *Mother Teresa: In My Own Words,* p. 19.

Cain's wife?" Mr. Sunday responded, "I honor every seeker after the truth. But I should like to warn this man that he shouldn't risk salvation by too many inquiries after other men's wives."[128]

• Bob Hope's wife Dolores is a devout Catholic. Once, she got on a plane in which two priests were seated in front of her and three nuns were seated behind her. Charlie Lee, one of Mr. Hope's many writers, was also on the plane. He asked Mr. Hope, "Why can't she take out regular insurance, like the rest of us?"[129]

Hypocrites

• Reed Smoot was one of the first Senators from Utah. He was a Mormon, and it was rumored that he was a polygamist, although he wasn't (however, he did support polygamy when that was Mormon doctrine). Mr. Smoot's swearing-in was delayed by a filibuster until another Senator looked at all the philanderers in the Senate, then said, "Gentlemen, I would rather have a polygamist who does not polyg, than a monogamist who does not monog."[130]

• A nobleman told the Bishop of Meaux, Jacques Bossuet, that he didn't go to church because there were too many hypocrites there. Bishop Bossuet responded, "Don't let that keep you away, my lord, because there is always room for one more."[131]

Ignorance

• Religion in the American frontier was often almost nonexistent, save for circuit-riding preachers, who were sometimes astonished by the ignorance of the people they were trying to teach. The Reverend Freeborn Garrettson, a Methodist circuit rider, asked a frontiersman, "Do you know Jesus Christ?" The frontiersman answered, "Sir, I do not know where the gentleman lives." To test a young boy's knowledge of Scripture, another circuit rider asked, "Who killed Abel?" The young boy answered, "I didn't know he was dead. We just moved here last week."[132]

• Rabbi Isaac Elhanan Spektor received a visit from a young man who was wondering whether he should give up his belief in God and become a free

---

128. Source: Lewis C. Henry, *Humorous Anecdotes About Famous People*, p. 71.
129. Source: Bob Hope, *The Road to Hollywood*, p. 38.
130. Source: Morris K. Udall, *Too Funny to be President*, p. 82.
131. Source: Lewis C. Henry, *Humorous Anecdotes About Famous People*, p. 70.
132. Source: Ross Phares, *Bible in Pocket, Gun in Hand*, pp. 1-2.

thinker. Rabbi Spektor asked whether the young man had read the Talmud. The answer came back: No. Had he read Maimonides? No. Had he read the Torah? No. Had he read Moses Mendelssohn? No. The Rabbi sighed and said, "Young man, you are too ignorant to call yourself a free thinker. You should call yourself by your correct name—an ordinary ignoramus."[133]

Marriage

• After a man and woman of Sidon had been married for 20 years without having any children, they were required by law to get a divorce. Rabbi Simeon ben Yohai told them that just as they had had a festive banquet when they got married, so now they should have one as they got a divorce. At the banquet, the husband told his wife that although he was divorcing her, she could have whatever she valued most in what had been their house. That night, as he slept, his divorced wife ordered her servants to remove him from his house to the house of her father. When her divorced husband woke up, he asked, "Where am I?" She told him, and when he asked why he was there, she replied, "Don't you remember your telling me last night that I may take with me whatever I like best when I return to my father's house? Nothing in the whole world do I like better than you!" They then went to Rabbi Simeon ben Yohai and remarried. (This time, she became pregnant, after the good Rabbi had prayed for her.)[134]

• A couple of Jewish painters were working inside a Catholic church when they became intrigued by a ritual. After asking what the ritual was, they learned that a nun was being prepared for the ceremony of professional—a ceremony that could be likened to a wedding between the nun and Jesus. After asking permission, the Jews were allowed to be present at the actual ceremony, but a surprised priest asked what they were doing there. The Jews replied, "We're relatives of the groom."[135]

• A Quaker thought about proposing, but hesitated because he wanted to make the right decision. However, while having tea at his loved one's house, he asked for half a cup of tea, and she filled his cup exactly half full. This so pleased the Quaker that he proposed. Years after they were married, his wife asked him why he had decided to propose to her. He explained the matter of the half a cup of tea, and she replied, "I remember that afternoon well—there wasn't another drop in the teapot."[136]

133. Source: Lawrence J. Epstein, *A Treasury of Jewish Anecdotes*, p. 219.
134. Source: Jakob J. Petuchowski, translator and editor, *Our Masters Taught*, pp. 92-93.
135. Source: Bill Adler, *Jewish Wit and Wisdom*, p. 132.

• Abraham Lincoln liked to tell a story about a soon-to-be justice of the peace who gave a marriage certificate to two people although he had not yet been authorized to hold office. The "marriage" certificate read: "To all the world Greeting. Know ye that John Smith and Peggy Myres is hereby certified to go together and do as old folks does, anywhere inside coperas precinct, and when my commission comes I am to marry them good and date em back to kivver accidents."[137]

• In the old days, women frequently died in childbirth, and their husbands remarried quickly. Only a few months after his first wife had died, Methodist preacher Joshua Thomas, aka "the Parson of the Islands," proposed marriage to a young woman. She asked, "Isn't this rather sudden?" He replied, "But I've had my eye on you for quite a while."[138]

• After Sydney Smith was married, he tossed six worn teaspoons into his bride's lap, then he explained that he had just fulfilled one of his marriage vows—he had endowed his wife with all his worldly goods.[139]

Mass

• Kathleen O'Connell Chesto tells this story about attending Mass with her two-year-old daughter, Liz. In his homily, the priest described Solomon's Temple as "magnificent." Liz recognized the word, so she stood up and told the congregation, "My Daddy calls me magnificent." The priest stopped his homily and said to the congregation, "Isn't that what being a Christian is all about? Each of us can say that we have a Daddy Who thinks that we are magnificent."[140]

• Three major league umpires, Tom Gorman, Augie Donatelli, and Artie Gore, went to Mass. Afterward, the three umpires and the priest, Father John, were standing outside the church when Milwaukee shortstop Johnny Logan walked by. Father John said to Mr. Logan, "How nice to see you. Do you see my three umpires? They all went to Mass and hit the rail. How about you?" Mr. Logan replied, "Father, they need it."[141]

• Pope John XXIII was the son of winegrowers, and he knew and appreciated good wine. After tasting some new wine from the Vatican vineyards, he joked with the papal gardener, "Enrico, do me the favor of not allowing any of the

136. Source: William H. Sessions, collector, *More Quaker Laughter*, p. 32.
137. Source: H. Allen Smith, *People Named Smith*, p. 105.
138. Source: Helen Chappell, *The Chesapeake Book of the Dead*, p. 31.
139. Source: H. Allen Smith, *People Named Smith*, p. 245.
140. Source: Kathleen O'Connell Chesto, *Why Are the Dandelions Weeds?*, pp. 15-16.
141. Source: Tom Gorman and Jerome Holtzman, *Three and Two!*, p. 124.

priests who come here to taste this wine. The Monsignors will all want to have it for their Masses, and then they might want to say Mass four or five times a day!"[142]

Money

• As a Methodist preacher in Texas, Edwin Porter attended Annual Conference each year, where he found out to which church he would be assigned for the following year and where stewards voted on allocating funds to worthy projects. One such project was the bishops' fund, but when discussion arose on this important topic, one steward didn't hear the final letter of the word "fund." The steward stood up and said, "Now, Brother Porter, I want to be a good member of the church and pay my part, but there's one thing I'm not willing to contribute to—that's the bishop's fun. Why can't the bishop pay for his own fun?"[143]

• Comedian Eddie Cantor was getting ready to star at one of the many benefits he supported to raise money for Israel. At this particular benefit, the admission was the purchase of a $1,000 Israel bond per person. On an elevator, Mr. Cantor happened to overhear an elderly couple talking about the benefit, which they were going to attend. The husband whispered to the wife, "Think of it. It's costing us $2,000 for this dinner today." The wife whispered back to the husband, "See, I'm telling you, Sam, it's costing more and more to eat out these days."[144]

• Lillian Baylis of the Old Vic and Sadler's Wells knew how to get people to work for her cheap. First, she would get on her knees and pray to God: "Please, God, send me a good tenor. And let him be cheap." After the tenor had asked for more money than she was prepared to pay, she would say, "You are asking for more money? Just a minute, dear. I will have to ask God." As the tenor stood in her office, she would get on her knees again and pray to God, then she would stand up and tell the tenor, "I'm sorry, dear. God says 'No.'"[145]

• Mulla Nasrudin was sitting upstairs when a beggar knocked at his door. Nasrudin poked his head outside the window and asked, "What do you want?" The beggar replied, "Come downstairs and I will tell you." Nasrudin went downstairs, where the beggar asked Nasrudin for alms. Nasrudin said, "Follow me," then he and the beggar went upstairs, where Nasrudin answered, "No." "Why did you

---

142. Source: Kurt Klinger, *A Pope Laughs*, p. 75.
143. Source: Alyene Porter, *Papa was a Preacher*, p. 72.
144. Source: Joey Adams, *The Borscht Belt*, p. 173.
145. Source: Margot Fonteyn, *Autobiography*, p. 36.

drag me upstairs?" asked the beggar. Nasrudin replied, "For the same reason you dragged me downstairs."[146]

• W.C. Fields got his first paying juggling job in 1891, when the deacon of a Methodist church agreed to pay him and a friend 30 cents to perform their act at a festival hosted by the church. However, after the act, the Methodist deacon refused to pay the money. This made Mr. Fields and his friend so angry that they stole 31 umbrellas from the Methodist church and pawned them for $1.20. After this unfortunate experience, Mr. Fields formed the resolution to do his act only for Baptists.[147]

• Gregor Mendel, whose research on peas led to the development of the science of genetics, joined the Order of Saint Augustine and eventually became the abbot at his monastery in Brünn, Moravia. One of the reasons the other monks elected him as abbot was that the government taxed the monastery each time it elected a new abbot and therefore it preferred to elect young abbots, such as the 45-year-old Father Mendel, who would probably live for many years.[148]

• Elias Hicks, a Quaker farmer, once had an abundant wheat crop when his neighbors' fields did poorly. Speculators knew that the price of wheat would rise, and they offered to buy Mr. Hicks' crop at a high price, but he declined to sell. Later, when his neighbors began to suffer from the effects of the poor growing season, Mr. Hicks sold them wheat—but at the normal price, not at the higher price.[149]

Monks

• According to legend, the monks who studied at the Shaolin Temple had a unique graduation ceremony. They were sent to the temple's maze of underground passageways and had to find their way out by passing many tests. In one test, the monk came to a wall on which were hanging many weapons, a broom, and a sign saying, "Choose one." The monk would select one, then go into the next room, which turned out to be filled with scorpions. If the monk had chosen the broom, he was able to simply sweep the scorpions out of his way. Getting through the room was much more difficult if the monk had chosen a sword. At the end of the underground passageways, one final door needed to be opened, and the only way to open it was to use one's bare arms to lift and move a searingly

146. Source: Charles Downing, *Tales of the Hodja*, p. 75.
147. Source: Jack Mingo, *The Juicy Parts*, p. 113.
148. Source: Roger Klare, *Gregor Mendel: Father of Genetics*, p. 72.
149. Source: Irvin C. Poley and Ruth Verlenden Poley, *Friendly Anecdotes*, pp. 93-94.

hot cauldron decorated on each side with dragon designs. In moving the caul-dron, the monk's graduation diploma—the figures of the dragon—were burned into his arms.[150]

• Two monks and a woman crossed a river on a ferry. One monk ogled the woman, then he winked to his companion, so the woman slapped him. The monk then closed his eyes, but a few minutes later the woman slapped him again. The monk said, "What have I done wrong? I had my eyes closed!" The woman said, "You have been thinking about me with your eyes closed—and that is worse than ogling me with your eyes open!"[151]

Mothers

• Before one seeks truth in faraway places, one ought to find the truth that is available at home. Yang Pu wished to study Buddhism under a great Buddhist teacher, so he left his home and went to Sichuan Province. However, he met an old man to whom he confided his ambition. But the old man asked, "Wouldn't it be better to seek Buddha rather than a teacher?" "Of course," said Yang Pu, "but where is Buddha to be found?" The old man said, "Go home. When you see a person wearing a blanket and with shoes on the wrong feet, that person is Bud-dha." Yang Pu returned home, where his mother heard him. She was so happy that he was home that she threw a blanket around herself and put on her shoes so hurriedly that she put them on the wrong feet.[152]

• When Dovid Goldwasser acted as Rabbi at a summer camp in Poland for Jewish adults, he met many people who had stories to tell about the Nazis and the death camps. One man, Boruch Segal, told about being lined up to be deported to Buchenwald by the Nazis. A mother in line, who was not observant as a Jew, saw a Rabbi and ran over to him so he could bless her infant daughter. The Rabbi blessed her daughter, saying, "May your daughter live a long life and may she one day become a leader of her community." After telling this story to Rabbi Gold-wasser, Mr. Segal pointed to a woman nearby—a leader of one of the groups at the camp—and said, "*She* was that baby."[153]

150. Source: Luana Metil and Jace Townsend, *The Story of Karate: From Buddhism to Bruce Lee*, p. 24.
151. Source: Alexei D. Voskressenski, compiler and editor, *Cranks, Knaves, and Jokers of the Celestial*, pp. 102-103.
152. Source: Chih-Chung Tsai (editor and illustrator) and Kok Kok Kiang (translator), *The Book of Zen*, p. 30.
153. Source: Rabbi Dovid Goldwasser, *It Happened in Heaven*, pp. 156-157.

• When Kathleen O'Connell Chesto was a young girl, she looked into a mirror and complained about a perceived lack of beauty. Her mother overheard her complaints, then told her, "Don't you dare criticize my handiwork!"[154]

Movies

• One of the studio heads at Paramount invited Groucho Marx to a screening of *Samson and Delilah*, starring the muscular Victor Mature and the beautiful Dorothy Lamarr, then the studio head asked Groucho how he liked the movie. Groucho pointed out the one glaring fault the movie had: "No picture can hold my interest where the leading man's bust is bigger than the leading lady's." For a long time thereafter, Groucho wasn't invited to screenings at Paramount.[155]

• At the end of the movie *Schindler's List*, many Jews saved by Oskar Schindler are shown placing stones on his burial marker. This is a Jewish tradition—the stones symbolize that the memory of this man will not be blown away by the wind.[156]

Nazis

• One form of resistance against the Nazis was the telling of jokes. (The powerful never like to be mocked.) In one story, Nazi propagandist Paul Joseph Goebbels toured a school where he asked the children for patriotic slogans. One student shouted, "*Heil Hitler!*" Goebbels was pleased and said, "Very good." Another student shouted, "*Deutschland über alles.*" Goebbels was again pleased, but asked, "How about a stronger slogan than these?" A small boy raised his hand, then declared, "Our people shall live forever." "Excellent," Goebbels said. "That is indeed a stronger slogan than the others. What's your name, little boy?" The boy replied, "Israel Goldberg."[157]

• Billy Wilder, the Jewish-American film director, served with the United States Army Psychological Warfare Division during World War II. After the war, some Germans wrote him for permission to put on a play depicting the crucifixion of Jesus Christ. After investigating the Germans, Mr. Wilder discovered that they had been either storm troopers or members of the Gestapo. Therefore, Mr. Wilder said that he would give them permission to put on the play—as long as they used real nails.[158]

---

154. Source: Kathleen O'Connell Chesto, *Why Are the Dandelions Weeds?*, p. 134.
155. Source: Groucho Marx, *Groucho and Me*, p. 324.
156. Source: Tom Powers, *Steven Spielberg: Master Storyteller*, p. 101.
157. Source: Steve Lipman, *Laughter in Hell*, p. 172.

• Josef Müller was a Catholic priest in Grossdungen who was sentenced to death for telling an anti-Nazi joke. Father Müller told about a dying German soldier who asked to have a photograph of Adolf Hitler placed on one side of him and a photograph of Gestapo head Hermann Goering placed on the other. When he was asked why, he replied, "That way I can die like Jesus—between two thieves."[159]

Peace

• Betty Williams was born in Belfast, Northern Ireland, and in general she was in favor of the activities of the Irish Republican Army until the day she saw a young British soldier get shot and die. As he lay dying, she knelt beside him and they prayed together. In 1976, she and Mairead Corrigan won the Nobel Peace Prize for their efforts to stop the violence in Northern Ireland.[160]

• John Roberts, a Quaker in New Jersey, was going by the market place, when he stooped to tie his shoe. As he did so, a man hit him in the back and said, "Take that for Jesus' sake!" Mr. Roberts didn't look back at the man; instead, he merely straightened up and said, "So I do," then continued on his way. A couple of days later, the man who had hit him begged to be forgiven.[161]

People with Handicaps

• As a person with cerebral palsy, which affects his motor skills, Cordell Brown learned to put other people at ease. At a church camp, Mr. Brown knew that the other campers were uneasy with his cerebral palsy. After unsuccessfully trying several times to plug in his electric razor, he turned to the other campers and said, "Just call me speed and coordination." The other campers laughed; after that, Mr. Brown became friends with them.[162]

• Mentally retarded people can be religious, too. To prepare for her Bat Mitzvah, Leslie Fish, who became mentally retarded after suffering from meningitis as a baby, studied Hebrew for five years—which she says was "hard." She wrote her own speech for the ceremony; in her speech, she talked about being responsible for her actions.[163]

---

158. Source: Rabbi Joseph Telushkin, *Jewish Humor*, p. 116.

159. Source: Steve Lipman, *Laughter in Hell*, p. 34.

160. Source: Anne Schraff, *Women of Peace: Nobel Peace Prize Winners*, p. 51.

161. Source: Helen White Charles, collector and editor, *Quaker Chuckles*, pp. 32-33.

162. Source: Cordell Brown, *I am What I am by the Grace of God*, p. 94.

163. Source: Martha McNey, *Leslie's Story*, pp. 26-27.

Perspective

• Rabbi Shlomo Carlebach took his message to everyone, including the very poor and even the mentally disturbed. He delivered a talk to Manhattan's Diamond Dealers' Club, where a man asked, "Shlomo, we love your music and your Hasidic tales are also very nice, but there's one thing that bothers some of us and which we just can't understand: Why are you always so busy with low-lifes and crazies?" Rabbi Shlomo replied that he knew he was among diamond experts, and he asked if any of them had ever thrown away a million-dollar diamond because it was a diamond in the rough. The diamond dealers laughed and said that none of them would ever do that. Rabbi Shlomo then said, "My sweetest friends, please try to remember this because it's the most important thing to know in life. Everyone—*everyone*—is a diamond in the rough."[164]

• A woman continually cried, no matter what the weather was like. If it rained, she cried. If it was sunny, she cried. When she was asked why she continually cried, she explained that she had two daughters. One daughter was married to a shoe salesman and the other daughter was married to an umbrella salesman. The woman cried when it was raining because no one would go out into the rain and buy shoes, and she cried when it was sunny because no one would bother to buy an umbrella. A wise person asked her why she didn't smile when it rained because it meant that people would buy umbrellas, and why she didn't smile when it was sunny because it meant that people would buy shoes. After that, no matter what the weather was like, the old woman smiled.[165]

Poor

• The motherhouse of Mother Teresa's Missionaries of Charity had no stoves, no washing machines, no electric fans, no air conditioners. Mother Teresa explained, "I do not want them. The poor we serve have none." When she first had the idea of starting the Missionaries of Charity, she even thought that she would allow the nuns to eat only the kind of food the very poorest people ate—rice and salt. However, she asked advice from Mother Dengal, who told her, "How do you expect your sisters to work, if their bodies receive no sustenance?" As a result of the advice, Mother Teresa allowed her nuns to eat well, but to eat only simple food.[166]

---

164. Source: Yitta Halberstam Mandelbaum, *Holy Brother*, pp, 19-20.
165. Source: Chih-Chung Tsai, *Zen Speaks*, p. 62.
166. Source: Amy Ruth, *Mother Teresa*, pp. 55-56, 68.

• During years of interviewing children for his TV program *House Party*, Art Linkletter occasionally interviewed an underprivileged child. (Mr. Linkletter himself grew up in a poor family. He writes in *Kids Say the Darnest Things!* that if the church hadn't donated dinners to his family, holidays such as Thanksgiving and Christmas would have been bleak.) In one interview, he asked an impoverished child, "What makes a happy home?" The little boy answered, "A steady paycheck."[167]

• In an inn, a rich man mistook Rebbe Zusia for a beggar and mistreated him. However, when he discovered that it was Rebbe Zusia he was mistreating, and not a beggar, he asked Zusia for forgiveness. Rebbe Zusia replied, "You have treated Zusia with respect; it is a poor beggar that you have mistreated. Go and ask forgiveness from beggars everywhere."[168]

Practical Jokes

• Lorenzo Dow was a traveling evangelist in the old days. At a camp meeting, he met a preacher who had a habit of ending every sermon with the cry, "Hurry up, Gabriel, and blow your horn!" Therefore, the Reverend Dow hired a boy to hide in a tall tree before the preacher's sermon, and at the conclusion of the sermon, while hidden by the tree's leaves, to blow on a hunting horn.[169]

• Gregor Mendel, whose work with peas led to the development of the science of genetics, was a priest in the Order of Saint Augustine. Priests aren't supposed to have children, but Father Mendel enjoyed shocking visitors to his monastery by telling them, "Now I am going to show you my children." He would then lead the visitors to his garden and show them his pea plants.[170]

• Mark Twain listened to a sermon, then he told the preacher that he had at home a book that contained every word of the preacher's sermon. This astonished and worried the preacher because he did not want to be guilty of even unintentional plagiarism. He asked to see a copy of the book, and Mr. Twain sent it to him—it was a dictionary.[171]

---

167. Source: Art Linkletter, *Kids Say the Darndest Things!*, p. 105.
168. Source: Elie Wiesel, *Souls on Fire*, p. 126.
169. Source: H. Allen Smith, *The Compleat Practical Joker*, p. 83.
170. Source: Roger Klare, *Gregor Mendel: Father of Genetics*, p. 45.
171. Source: H. Allen Smith, *The Compleat Practical Joker*, p. 28.

Prayer

• Art Rooney felt that he had gotten a good price when he bought the Pittsburgh Steelers partly because his two sisters were nuns and his brother was a priest. Another person with a religious connection was Joe Paterno, coach of Penn State. When Penn State was having a big winning streak, his mother would listen to the games, and if Penn State was losing, she would go into the bathroom with her rosary and pray. In the Orange Bowl, Kansas led Penn State for most of the game, and with Mr. Paterno's mother in the bathroom praying, Penn State scored to come within one point, 14-13. Mr. Paterno decided to go for a win with a two-point conversion, but the attempt failed. With his mother still praying, a referee called a penalty on Kansas for having too many players on the field, and on its second attempt, Penn State made the two-point conversion to win by one point. After the game, Mr. Paterno received a telegram from Mr. Rooney: "Congratulations. I'll trade you my brother and two sisters for your mother, straight up."[172]

• A deeply religious woman was shocked when her 14-year-old son revealed that he was gay, and so she did what deeply religious people should do—she prayed for guidance. Very quickly, she received an answer to her prayers. God said to her, "You know what a gay person is like; you lived with one for 14 years." After hearing that, she decided that the problem was not homosexuality, but some people's negative reaction to homosexuality. She says, "From that moment on, I never shed another tear that my son was gay. I may have shed a lot of tears for how he was treated, but not because he was gay." (The woman's husband quickly accepted his son's homosexuality, saying simply, "He's a nice boy, and I love him.")[173]

• In 1962, in *Engel v. Vitale*, the United States Supreme Court ruled against allowing a nondenominational prayer to be recited in New York Public Schools. It was a controversial decision, but many people supported it. President John F. Kennedy expressed the opinion that children could learn about prayer much more meaningfully at home and in church. Many religious leaders expressed the opinion that nondenominational prayers, such as the one that had been recited in the New York City schools, were bland, vague, and almost meaningless—hardly the stuff of real prayer.[174]

---

172. Source: Joe Garagiola, *It's Anybody's Ballgame*, pp. 106-107.
173. Source: Chastity Bono, *Family Outing*, pp. 216-217.
174. Source: J. Edward Evans, *Freedom of Religion*, pp. 50-52.

• For much of his political career, Alabama politician George Wallace was a strict segregationist, but eventually he changed and admitted that he had been wrong about segregation. In 1987, Reverend Jesse Jackson went to Mr. Wallace's home, and Mr. Wallace asked, "Would you pray for me?" They joined hands, and Reverend Jackson prayed for him. According to Mr. Wallace's son, both Mr. Wallace and Reverend Jackson had tears in their eyes. At the end of the prayer, Mr. Wallace told Reverend Jackson, "Jesse, I love you." Reverend Jackson replied, "Governor, I love you, too."[175]

• In 1982, Lebanon and Israel were in conflict. Mother Teresa traveled to Lebanon, where she asked to be allowed to take care of disabled children still present in hospitals that had been bombed. The authorities did not see what she would be able to accomplish during a time of fighting, so they asked her to wait for a ceasefire to start doing her good works. Mother Teresa prayed, and the very next day a ceasefire was declared. She then took the disabled children to East Beirut, where the Missionaries of Charity had a home and could take care of them.[176]

• In the first half of the 20th century, Ed Diddle coached the football team of Western Kentucky State Teachers College—the Praying Colonels. Mr. Diddle once coached his team captain in how to say a prayer properly—one should ask for one's team to give a good performance on the playing field, but one should not ask for victory. Before the game, the team captain started to pray, but in the middle of the prayer, Mr. Diddle interrupted: "Damn it! I told you not to ask for victory!"[177]

• George Burns was not an observant Jew as an adult because of something that happened when he was a child. His grandmother died, and his family needed to have a *minyan*—a group of 10 Jews to pray and hold services. Unfortunately, his family was able to get only seven Jews—so they had to pay three other Jews to pray in the *minyan*. Mr. Burns says, "That stuck with me all my life. I couldn't imagine anyone getting paid for praying."[178]

• Rabbi Bunam prayed quietly, but in his youth Rabbi Hanokh of Alexandria prayed loudly with many gestures. Rabbi Hanokh was praying loudly when Rabbi Bunam entered the synagogue. Immediately, Rabbi Hanokh grew quiet, then he told himself that he should be concerned about God, not about Rabbi

175. Source: Michael A. Schuman, *Martin Luther King: Leader for Civil Rights*, pp. 112-113.
176. Source: Amy Ruth, *Mother Teresa*, p. 89.
177. Source: Fred Russell, *I'll Try Anything Twice*, p. 14.
178. Source: Tim Boxer, *The Jewish Celebrity Hall of Fame*, p. 48.

Bunam, so he began to pray loudly again. After Rabbi Hanokh's loud prayer, Rabbi Bunam told him that he was especially pleased by the prayer.[179]

• In 1933, an earthquake struck Los Angeles. Two members of the New York Giants organization—manager Bill Terry and club secretary Jim Tierney—were rooming together. When the quake struck, Mr. Tierney, a devout Catholic, knelt and prayed. Mr. Terry, who was not a devout Catholic, also knelt, saying, "I don't know what you're saying, Tierney, but it goes for me, too."[180]

• George Washington said grace at his table although a clergyman was dining with him. After the clergyman had left, Mr. Washington's wife told him that he should have asked the clergyman to say grace. Mr. Washington expressed regret, then added, "The reverend gentleman will at least be assured that we are not entirely graceless at Mount Vernon."[181]

• A little girl had been naughty, so she was sent to her room for a quiet time. Afterward, all smiles, she returned to her family, saying, "I prayed to God." "That's good," said her mother. "Did you pray that God would help you be a good girl?" "No," she replied. "I prayed that God would help you put up with me."[182]

• When Mark Twain was dying, a relative wrote him to say that she had asked some nuns to pray for him. Mr. Twain wrote back, "I am grateful for the prayers of those good nuns and for yours; they have already answered themselves in giving me a deep pleasure."[183]

• Edward Everett Hale used to be Chaplain of the United States Senate. He was asked, "When you look at the state of our country, do you pray for the Senators in your charge?" He replied, "No—when I look at our Senators, I pray for our country."[184]

• Comedian Lou Costello's mother was Catholic, and she often prayed in the Catholic Church. However, on occasion she also prayed in a nearby synagogue, saying, "It's closer to home, and I can pray there just as well."[185]

• If you ever watch gardeners, you will realize that a common weed sometimes accomplishes what God does not—get people on their knees.[186]

---

179. Source: William B. Silverman, *Rabbinic Wisdom and Jewish Values*, p. 71.
180. Source: Fred Russell, *I'll Try Anything Twice*, p. 43.
181. Source: P.M. Zall, *George Washington Laughing*, p. 30.
182. Source: Beulah Collins, collector, *For Benefit of Clergy*, p. 17.
183. Source: Cyril Clemens, "Mark Twain's Religion," p. 12.
184. Source: Dick Hyman, *Potomac Wind and Wisdom*, pp. 50-52.
185. Source: Bob Thomas, *Bud & Lou*, p. 39.
186. Source: Ivy Moody, *Illustrations with a Point*, p. 14.

Preachers

• Lyndon Baines Johnson used to enjoy telling a story about a man who habitually napped during church services. One day the preacher got tired of the man's napping, so he told the congregation, "If you want to go to Heaven, please stand up." Everyone in the congregation—except the sleeping man—stood up. After the preacher asked everyone to sit down, he said in his normal voice, "If you want to go to Hell," then he shouted, "STAND UP!" The sleeping man woke up and immediately jumped to his feet, only to look around and see that the rest of the congregation were sitting. So the man looked at the preacher and said, "I don't know what we're voting on, but it looks like you and I are the only ones in favor of it."[187]

• Some people go to great lengths to protect the health of their pastor. Wesleyan preacher William Woughter received a telephone call from a woman who wanted him to go to a hospital and pray with her father. The woman explained that she had gotten his name from a relative who attended his church, and she would have asked her own pastor to pray with her father—except that her father had a highly communicable disease that she didn't want her own pastor to catch. Yes, Pastor William did go to the hospital to pray with the woman's father, and no, he didn't catch the highly communicable disease.[188]

• When St. Patrick was speaking about the Trinity—the doctrine that there is only one God, who is Father, Son, and Holy Ghost—someone asked what sense it made to believe in only one God and yet believe God is Father, Son, and Holy Ghost. St. Patrick bent down and plucked a shamrock—a leaf of the clover plant. He displayed it and showed that it was only one leaf, yet it had three parts. The three parts of the one shamrock leaf correspond to the three parts of the one God. Since then, the shamrock has been a symbol of St. Patrick.[189]

• Preacher George Whitefield and a friend were staying at an inn where they were disturbed by gamblers in the next room. Mr. Whitefield felt that gambling was a sin and so he went next door and remonstrated with the gamblers about their behavior, then he returned to his room and prepared for bed. His criticisms had no effect, for the people next door continued gambling, so his friend asked what he had received for his trouble. Mr. Whitefield replied, "A soft pillow," then he went to sleep.[190]

187. Source: Dick Hyman, *Potomac Wind and Wisdom*, p. 40.
188. Source: William Woughter, *All Preachers of Our God & King*, pp. 62-63.
189. Source: Dorothy Rhodes Freeman, *St. Patrick's Day*, p. 32.
190. Source: J. Vernon Jacobs, compiler, *450 True Stories from Church History*, p. 107.

• The early 19th century Philadelphia lawyer Nicholas Waln was a Quaker. Of course, he lived long before air conditioning. On a stifling hot day, he served as head of a meeting and he chose to end the meeting very early. This shocked his fellow Quakers. When they asked why he had ended the meeting so early, he referred to the words of the prophet Hosea: "I desire mercy and not burnt offerings."[191]

• As a young reporter, H.L. Mencken covered each Sunday the sermon given by Cardinal Gibbons. Very quickly, he learned that the Cardinal gave essentially the same sermon each Sunday, so one Sunday he didn't bother to attend the sermon, but merely sent in the usual copy to his newspaper. That happened to be the Sunday that Cardinal Gibbons gave a rousing sermon that ended up on the front page.[192]

• Reverend Andrew Jumper was the pastor of Central Presbyterian Church in Clayton, Missouri, and one year he was hired to go to spring training to give weekly services to professional baseball players. After one sermon, a player told him, "God gave you a great sermon today." Reverend Jumper replied, "Yes, but I want you to know I typed it."[193]

• When he was elderly, Church of Christ preacher T.B. Larimore preached the same sermon two nights in a row. When his wife told him, "You preached that sermon last night," he was unperturbed and replied, "It's a good one."[194]

Prejudice

• The mother of James Augustine Healy was Eliza Clark, a black slave in Georgia. Mr. Healy became a priest, and in 1875, he became second bishop of Portland, Maine. Occasionally, his race caused awkward moments. While hearing one young girl's confession, Mr. Healy was surprised when she stopped and said, "I can't tell you the rest of my sins." When Mr. Healy asked why, she replied, "Because it's something I said against the bishop." After finally learning that she had said that the bishop was as black as the devil, Mr. Healy told her, "Oh, my child, don't say the bishop is as black as the devil. You can say he's as black as coal, or as black as the ace of spades, but don't say he's as black as the devil!" During another confession, a young boy told Mr. Healy, "…and I called the bishop a nigger!" Mr. Healy opened the confessional curtain so the boy could

191. Source: Chuck Fager, *Quakers are Funny!*, pp. 81-82.
192. Source: Jim Tully, *A Dozen and One*, p. 231.
193. Source: Joe Garagiola, *It's Anybody's Ballgame*, p. 97.
194. Source: Gary Holloway, *Saints, Demons, and Asses*, p. 66.

see him and said, "Well, son, is there anything wrong with being a nigger? Take a good look at your bishop. Is there anything wrong with being a nigger?"[195]

• Butterfly McQueen, an African-American actress, played Jack Benny's maid, but eventually she quit, apparently because some people felt she was demeaning herself by playing a maid—although she was making a large salary *playing* a maid at a time when many people of color were making a small salary *being* maids. Mr. Benny protested, "Good grief! I'm paying Butterfly $750 a week [big money at the time]. Where else can she get that kind of money? Besides, everybody loves her. I don't think she's demeaning herself." Mr. Benny paused, thought a moment about the other woman on his show, Mary Livingston, his on-radio girlfriend and real-life wife, then he asked, "What does Butterfly want to do—play Mary's sister?" A moment later, he smiled and answered his own question, "No. She wouldn't want to do *that*. Mary's Jewish."[196]

• Country comedian Jerry Clower grew up in Mississippi at a time when white people grew up with the attitude that they were better than black people. Fortunately, he was able to unlearn bigotry. When black student James Meredith enrolled in the University of Mississippi, the state government did not encourage citizens to keep control of their hatred. Disturbances broke out, fires were set on campus, and two people died. Mr. Clower, a Christian, got down on his knees in his bedroom and prayed, "Oh, dear God, if my attitude has caused some people to react to this situation like this, I hereby re-dedicate my life. I'm going to change, because I don't want to encourage an attitude that would cause people to break the law, kill folks, or keep a qualified student from entering the University of Mississippi."[197]

• At one time, actors and theaters were regarded as sinful. After an actor named George Holland died, the great 19th-century actor Joseph Jefferson went to a church in New York to arrange for a funeral, but the clergyman told him that actors could not have funerals in that church; however, he did say that "a little church around the corner" was willing to hold funerals for actors. "The Little Church Around the Corner" is the Church of the Transfiguration, located on East Twenty-ninth Street. The critic Edward Wagenknecht says that it is "a living testimonial against bigotry and a living protest against the tendency to regard human beings as members of groups rather than as themselves."[198]

195. Source: John Deedy, *A Book of Catholic Anecdotes*, p. 112.
196. Source: Glenhall Taylor, *Before Television*, pp. 113, 115.
197. Source: Jerry Clower, *Life Everlaughter*, p. 44.
198. Source: Edward Wagenknecht, *Merely Players*, pp. 204-205.

• "Shoeless Joe" Jackson was tossed out of professional baseball after the 1919 Black Sox scandal, when he was charged with helping the Black Sox throw the World Series, although he batted .375 in the series. This disgrace stayed with him for the rest of his life. Back home in South Carolina, he and his wife, Katie, offered to buy an organ for the Brandon Methodist Church they attended, but the church turned down the money on account of the scandal, despite having accepted tithes from the couple for many years. Therefore, "Shoeless Joe" and Katie began attending the Brandon Baptist Church and bought it an organ.[199]

• In 1928, Tom Connally and Earle B. Mayfield ran against each other in a campaign to be elected to the United States Senate. The Ku Klux Klan, which was powerful in Texas in those days and which supported Mr. Mayfield, started rumors that in San Antonio Mr. Connally's daughter was attending a Catholic convent school. In addition to calling the KKK "un-American and devil-possessed," Mr. Connally showed that the KKK were liars by taking his only child, a son, to his political rallies, where he introduced him by saying, "Now, folks, this is my daughter, who is attending a Catholic convent school for girls in San Antonio."[200]

• Hung-jen, the Fifth Patriarch, met Hui-Neng, who was to become the Sixth Patriarch and who wanted to study with Hung-jen. The Fifth Patriarch asked, "Who are you, where are you from, and what do you want?" The Sixth Patriarch-to-be answered, "I am a commoner, I come from the south, and I have come here to become a Buddha." The Fifth Patriarch decided to test him by asking, "How can a southerner and a barbarian ever become a Buddha?" The Sixth Patriarch-to-be replied, "The Buddha-nature knows of no north or south, no monk or barbarian."[201]

• When Muriel, a lesbian, was in high school, her first close friend was a girl named Millie. After Millie was missing for a couple of days, Muriel discovered that she was absent from school because of a Jewish holiday. Muriel had not realized that Millie was Jewish before, and that got her thinking about all the things that ignorant people say about people of other races, religions, or creeds. She felt that Millie was just like her, with many ideas in common, so she lost her prejudice fast.[202]

• Some Puritans absolutely despised the Native Americans, even though the Native Americans had helped the earliest European immigrants survive in the

199. Source: Joe Thompson, *Growing Up with "Shoeless Joe,"* pp. 122-123.
200. Source: John F. Parker, *"If Elected, I Promise…."*, p. 58.
201. Source: Robert E. Kennedy, *Zen Spirit, Christian Spirit*, p. 77.
202. Source: Zsa Zsa Gershick, *Gay Old Girls*, pp. 79-80.

new land. Cotton Mather, a prominent Puritan preacher, told his congregation that it was "the duty of good Christians to exterminate" the Native Americans. In addition to fighting the Native Americans, the Puritans occasionally captured some Native Americans and sold them into slavery.[203]

• During the Jim Crow days, a black couple wanted to move into a white-only neighborhood. Hearing this, an outraged Catholic wrote a petition to keep the black couple out, and he asked his next-door neighbor, a Protestant, to sign it. The Protestant, however, declined to sign the petition. Puzzled, the Catholic asked why. The Protestant replied, "Petitions don't work. Ten years ago, I signed a petition to keep *you* from moving into the neighborhood."[204]

• A black man went to a "whites only" church and was turned away at the door and told to go to the black church and pray to God there. The black man went back to the white church the following Sunday and said, "I took your advice. I prayed to God and He told me not to feel bad that I had been kept out of your church—He said that He's been trying to get into your church for years, and He hasn't made it yet."[205]

• Jewish comedian Lenny Bruce was in a diner on Sunset Boulevard when a tough-looking man got off his motorcycle, walked in, and said, "I'm gonna kill me every Jew in this place." Mr. Bruce immediately began singing, "When Israel was in Egypt land, let my people go." He got the worst of the fight, but he amused police officers with his comedy when they arrived to stop the disturbance.[206]

• Morris K. Udall, a Mormon and later a politician from Arizona, ran into bigotry while serving in the Army. An Army Major asked, "Morris? What kind of a name is that?" Later, Mr. Udall received a letter from "Judge Levi Udall," and immediately the Major thought that he was Jewish, so the Major began to treat him exactly like he treated all of his Jewish officers—badly.[207]

Public Speaking

• In the old days, many people regarded playing cards as irreligious. Susan B. Anthony, a Quaker, gave a speech in which she introduced a Methodist friend of hers, the Reverend Anna Howard Shaw, as her "right bower," thinking that a

---

203. Source: Anita Louise McCormick, *Native Americans and the Reservation in American History*, pp. 18-19, 30-31.
204. Source: Hiley H. Ward, editor, *Ecumania*, p. 71.
205. Source: Joey Adams, *The God Bit*, p. 252.
206. Source: Phil Berger, *The Last Laugh*, p. 86.
207. Source: Morris K. Udall, *Too Funny to be President*, p. 95.

right bower was a right-hand man and not knowing that a right bower is a lead-ing card in the game of euchre. The audience laughed, mystifying Ms. Anthony, until the meaning of "right bower" was explained to her later. The next day Ms. Anthony again addressed the audience, and she said, "When I came to your town, I had been warned that you were a very religious lot of people. I wanted to impress upon you that Miss Shaw and I are religious, too. But I admit that when I told you she was my right bower I did not know what a right bower was. I have learned that since last night." The audience laughed, then Ms. Anthony contin-ued, "It interests me very much, however, to realize that every one of you seemed to know all about a right bower, and that I had to come to your good orthodox town to get that information."[208]

• Cordell Brown says that having cerebral palsy can be an advantage in public speaking, which he has often done to raise money for Camp Echoing Hills, a camp he founded in Warsaw, Ohio, for adults with handicaps. Because the cere-bral palsy affects his speech and coordination, no one can tell when Mr. Brown is nervous. He sometimes used to put his hands in his pockets at the beginning of his fund-raising speech, then tell the audience, "I've got my hands in my pockets to start this presentation, because by the end of the evening, I'll have them in your pockets." Of course, having cerebral palsy does have disadvantages. Early one Saturday morning, Mr. Brown was at a car wash when a police car pulled in with its lights flashing. Someone had seen Mr. Brown washing his car, noticed that he was uncoordinated (an effect of cerebral palsy), thought he was drunk, and called the police![209]

• Some politicians change political parties. For example, Reverend W.H. Bill Alexander started out as a Democrat, but he changed his affiliation to Republi-can. In 1950, he ran against the junior senator from Oklahoma, A.S. Mike Mon-roney. Senator Monroney's senior colleague, Bob Kerr, campaigned for him. In a devastating reference to Reverend Alexander, Senator Kerr said, "Now, this fel-low Alexander one day said to his congregation, 'After communion with the Almighty, I have decided to enter the Democratic primaries and run for the Sen-ate.' Well, soon afterward, Alexander switched over and won the Republican nomination. What I'd like to know is this: If the Lord told Bill Alexander to run as a Democrat, who then told him to run as a Republican?"[210]

---

208. Source: Helen White Charles, collector and editor, *Quaker Chuckles*, pp. 12-13.
209. Source: Cordell Brown, *I am What I am by the Grace of God*, pp. 141-142, 197-198.
210. Source: John F. Parker, *"If Elected, I Promise...."*, p. 61.

Respect

• As a young boy, while in the Potala Palace, the 14th Dalai Lama enjoyed looking at people in the Tibetan capital city, Lhasa, through his telescope. Sometimes he looked at the people in the prison at the base of the hill the palace was situated on. Whenever the prisoners noticed that the Dalai Lama was looking at them through the telescope, they knelt to show him respect.[211]

• When Rumi, the founder of the Sufi order known as the Whirling Dervishes, died, many Jews and Christians showed up at his funeral. The Muslims were surprised that these non-Muslims wanted to attend the funeral of an eminent Muslim saint and sage, but they explained the great respect that they had for Rumi, and so they were allowed to attend his funeral.[212]

Sabbath

• Rabbi Shlomo Carlebach was an Orthodox Jew, and he never traveled by automobile on the Sabbath. Once, he was late for a Sabbath "happening" at a temple in Los Angeles. Night was falling, and he told the group he was traveling with that he had to get out and start walking because the Sabbath was starting. He and his group pulled their two cars over, got out, and started what turned out to be a 27-mile walk to the temple. News of their walk traveled quickly—a deejay called the Night Owl even interviewed Rabbi Shlomo and broadcast the interview during the walk—and several people joined them. At 4:30 a.m., they arrived at the temple. Rabbi Shlomo prayed, held the Friday night service, told stories, and taught Torah, and finally at 8:30 a.m. Saturday, he and his group sat down to the Sabbath meal. A person who was there said later, "For as long as I live, I will never forget that *Shabbos* with Shlomo Carlebach. Everyone who did that walk was transformed. We were a bunch of kids who didn't know anything about *Shabbos* until we took that walk, and this is how he taught us. After witnessing Shlomo Carlebach keeping *Shabbos* with such passion, devotion, and fervor…how could you not keep *Shabbos* after that?"[213]

• British actress Constance Benson sometimes toured in Scotland, whose inhabitants took the Sabbath seriously. For example, when she checked into a rooming house on the Sabbath, she was locked in her room and warned not to raise the blinds, as the landlady didn't want her neighbors to know that a "low play-actress" was staying in her house. Ms. Benson writes that the piano was

211. Source: Whitney Stewart, *The 14th Dalai Lama: Spiritual Leader of Tibet*, p. 52.
212. Source: Shams al-Din Ahmad Aflaki, *Legends of the Sufis*, pp. 86-87.
213. Source: Yitta Halberstam Mandelbaum, *Holy Brother*, pp. 9ff.

locked up on the Sabbath, but "there was generally a cheerful aroma of whiskey about the house."[214]

• A Teamster went to his Rabbi with a problem: His occupation frequently made it impossible for him to attend Sabbath services. The Rabbi listened, then asked, "While you are working, do you carry poor passengers free of charge?" The Teamster said that yes, he did. The Rabbi next said, "Then you serve the Lord in your occupation just as faithfully as I do when I am in the synagogue."[215]

Saints

• One of the most famous slaves in history is St. Patrick, who was kidnapped at age 16 in Britannia and taken away by pirates to Hibernia, which we know today as Ireland. He was bought by a chief named Miliuc, who made him a shepherd. For six years, Patrick remained a slave, until he heard a voice that told him, "Soon you will go to your own country. See, a ship is ready." He then escaped and walked 200 miles to the seashore, where he found a ship that was willing to take him to home and freedom. Later, of course, he returned to bring Christianity to Ireland and became a saint.[216]

• In 1431, English soldiers burned the French heroine Joan of Arc at the stake. After she died, the soldiers collected her ashes and threw them into the Seine River. However, the ashes of her heart were not thrown into the river because it had not burned even though the executioner swore that he had tried to burn it using charcoal, oil, and sulfur, in addition to the original wood. After she died, several people, including some English soldiers, became convinced that in killing Joan of Arc, they had killed a saint. In 1920, the Catholic Church made their fear a reality when it made her St. Joan.[217]

Scandals

• Muhammad Ali is a Muslim. Christian televangelist Jimmy Swaggart tried to convert him, but Mr. Ali declined to be converted, saying, "Think about it. If Jimmy Swaggart can convert the best-known Muslim on earth back to Christianity, what would that do for Jimmy Swaggart?" Soon afterward, Swaggart was involved in a sex scandal. One of Mr. Ali's friends suggested, "You really ought to

---

214. Source: Constance Benson, *Mainly Players*, pp. 38-39.
215. Source: Lawrence J. Epstein, *A Treasury of Jewish Anecdotes*, pp. 248-249.
216. Source: Dorothy Rhodes Freeman, *St. Patrick's Day*, pp. 13-15.
217. Source: Don Nardo, *The Trial of Joan of Arc*, pp. 80-82.

write Jimmy Swaggart a letter, saying that God still loves him and Jimmy Swaggart should accept Allah as his only lord and savior."[218]

• Pope John XXIII often took walks through the Vatican Gardens. To preserve the privacy of the Popes, the cupola of St. Peter's Basilica had been closed to the public, but the good Pope ordered it open to the public again, saying, "Why shouldn't the faithful watch me? I don't do anything that would give cause for scandal."[219]

Scripture

• One thing to learn from the Bible is that it is possible to bargain with God. When God wished to destroy Sodom, Abraham was upset because he did not think it was fair for the righteous to be destroyed with the wicked. Therefore, he asked God not to destroy Sodom if 50 righteous people were in the city. God agreed, then Abraham asked God not to destroy Sodom if 45 righteous people were in the city. God again agreed, so Abraham kept asking for mercy until God agreed not to destroy Sodom if only 10 righteous people were in the city. (Unfortunately, not even 10 righteous people were in Sodom, so it was destroyed—but not until the few righteous people had left the city.)[220]

• Two Rabbis, one of whom had many followers and one of whom had few followers, began talking. The first Rabbi, who had few followers, said that the other Rabbi had so many followers because the people thought that he could work wonders such as healing the sick and reading people's minds, then the first Rabbi asked if the other Rabbi knew what he was thinking. "Of course," said the Rabbi with many followers. "You are thinking of the verse in *Tehillim*, 'I have placed Hashem [God] before me always.'" "No," said the Rabbi with few followers. "I was not thinking of that verse." The Rabbi who had many followers said, "Then that's why you have so few followers."[221]

• A pastor read John 14:2 out of the New Testament, but he used a new translation which said, "In my Father's house there are many dwelling places." An elderly woman in the congregation stood up and said, "I want you to read that Scripture again—from my Bible. I've lived in old, run-down houses all my life, and I'm looking forward to that mansion!"[222]

218. Source: Jack Mingo, *The Juicy Parts*, p. 37.
219. Source: Henri Fesquet, collector, *Wit and Wisdom of Good Pope John*, pp. 44-45.
220. Source: Anthony Weston, *A Practical Companion to Ethics*, pp. 19-21.
221. Source: Shmuel Himelstein, *Words of Wisdom, Words of Wit*, p. 179.
222. Source: Edward K. Rowell, editor, *Humor for Preaching and Teaching*, p. 86.

• A homophobe said to lesbian comedian Judy Carter, "You can't be gay and be a Christian." She replied, "I must have a misprint in my Bible. It doesn't say, 'For God so loved the world that He gave His only begotten Son, that whosoever believeth in Him, *except homosexuals*, should not perish but have everlasting life.'"[223]

• When the Declaration of Independence was adopted on July 4, 1776, a man rang the bell of the meetinghouse to announce the news to the populace. On the Liberty Bell was engraved this quotation from the Bible: "Proclaim liberty throughout all the land unto all the inhabitants thereof."[224]

• Art Linkletter interviewed a little boy who was wearing a pin he had been awarded for going to Bible school for four years. When Mr. Linkletter asked him what his favorite Bible story was, the little boy answered, "Humpty Dumpty."[225]

Thanksgiving

• A rich racist Southern woman decided to have some soldiers over for Thanksgiving dinner, so she called the captain of the local Army base and said that she had room at her table for three soldiers—"but don't send over any Jews." Thanksgiving arrived, there was a knock at her door, and she opened it to find three black soldiers on the front porch. "Oh, no," she said, "there must be some mistake." "No, ma'am," said one of the soldiers politely. "Captain Abraham Goldstein never makes mistakes."[226]

• Two small girls were best friends—one girl was Jewish and the other girl was Christian. At Christmas, the Christian girl's grandfather asked her what her best friend had gotten for Christmas. The little girl replied, "She didn't get anything for Christmas. You see, I'm Christmas, and she's Chanukah. I'm Easter, and she's Passover. But we're both Thanksgiving."[227]

Theater

• In the 19th century, many clergymen looked down upon theaters and actors. One clergyman wanted to see the great actor Edwin Booth, so he wrote him to ask if Mr. Booth could arrange a way so he could see him act at Booth's

---

223. Source: Judy Carter, *The Homo Handbook*, p. 188.
224. Source: Leila Merrell Foster, *Benjamin Franklin: Founding Father and Inventor*, pp. 14-15.
225. Source: Art Linkletter, *I Didn't Do It Alone*, p. 94.
226. Source: Harvey Mindess, *The Chosen People?*, p. 83.
227. Source: Wayne Dosick, *Golden Rules*, pp. 58-59.

Theater without there being a chance that a member of his congregation would see him. Mr. Booth wrote back, saying, "There is no door in my theater through which God cannot see."[228]

• In rehearsals for *Fiddler on the Roof*, Zero Mostel kissed a mezuzah (a scroll of holy scriptures) which was nailed to a doorpost. Other people objected, saying that only a few people would understand what he was doing, so the next time Mr. Mostel came through the doorway, he made the sign of the cross. After that, he was allowed to kiss the mezuzah.[229]

Tobacco

• A Mennonite pastor punished his five-year-old son by removing him from church—an act the son felt was very unfair. To get revenge, the young boy waited until later in the day, when he and his father attended a men's business meeting, then the boy announced to the group, "My dad will probably deny this, but he smokes sometimes!"[230]

• One Church of Christ preacher, Jimmy Smith, caught another Church of Christ preacher, T.Q. Martin, smoking. Mr. Smith said, "I see you're burning incense to the devil." Mr. Martin replied, "Yes, but I didn't expect him to catch me at it."[231]

Wills

• Wilson Mizner, a rascal, led a life devoted to women, gambling, opium, and the spending of money—and he also devoted his life to wit. After he died, he made one last joke in his will: He left his estate to a woman. Everybody assumed, given the life Mr. Mizner had led, that the woman must have been his mistress, but she was a woman with whom he had had a Platonic friendship for the 15 years he knew her. The woman, Florence Atkinson, called him "the best and dearest friend I ever had in my whole life.…I know [his brother] Addison almost as well as Wilson. We were like three brothers."[232]

• Revolutionary War general Charles Lee made an infamous will which said, "I desire most earnestly that I may not be buried in any church, or church-yard,

228. Source: Edward Wagenknecht, *Merely Players*, p. 150.
229. Source: Kate Mostel and Madeline Gilford, *170 Years of Show Business*, pp. 166-167.
230. Source: Ken Alley, *Awkward Christian Soldiers*, p. 53.
231. Source: Gary Holloway, *Saints, Demons, and Asses*, p. 74.
232. Source: John Burke, *Rogue's Progress: The Fabulous Adventures of Wilson Mizner*, pp. 279-280.

or within a mile of any Presbyterian or Anabaptist meeting-house; for since I have resided in this country, I have kept so much bad company when living, that I do not chuse to continue it when dead."[233]

Wisdom

• Rabbi Joshua ben Hananiah was ugly, and the daughter of the Emperor of Rome told him that she thought it was odd that so ugly a man could have such wisdom. He then asked if the Emperor kept wine in earthen vessels. She replied that he did, and Rabbi Joshua told her that it was odd to keep such a good thing as wine in earthen vessels and that the Emperor ought to keep his wine in golden and silver vessels. She told the Emperor what Rabbi Joshua had said, and the Emperor ordered that his wine be kept in golden and silver vessels—but the golden and silver vessels turned the wine sour. Therefore, the Emperor called Rabbi Joshua before him. Rabbi Joshua explained what he and the Emperor's daughter had discussed, and he stated that he had merely repeated to the Emperor's daughter the same principle she had told to him—good things should not be kept in common vessels. The Emperor then asked, "Are there no handsome scholars?" Rabbi Joshua replied, "If the scholars were ugly, they would be even more scholarly."[234]

• A man planted flowers in his garden; however, when the flowers grew, dandelions also grew with them. The man sought advice from friends and tried several ways to get rid of the dandelions, but nothing worked. Finally, the man sought advice from a wise gardener. The wise gardener suggested several ways to get rid of the dandelions, but the man had already tried them. Finally, the wise gardener said, "I suggest that you learn to love dandelions."[235]

• Many people are in despair over their evil deeds, but instead of turning from evil and doing good, they continue to despair although they instead "could be stringing pearls for the delight of Heaven," in the words of the Rabbi of Ger. That is why the good Rabbi said, "It is written: 'Depart from evil and do good'—turn wholly from evil, do not dwell upon it, and do good. You have done wrong? Then counteract it by doing right."[236]

• During a sea voyage, a storm raged. A passenger on ship began to scream for help, and his shrieking disturbed the other passengers, who asked the wise Bahlul

233. Source: P.M. Zall, *George Washington Laughing*, p. 9.
234. Source: Nahum N. Glatzer, editor, *Hammer on the Rock*, pp. 19-20.
235. Source: Wayne Dosick, *Golden Rules*, pp. 142-143.
236. Source: Martin Buber, *The Way of Man*, p. 33.

what could be done to quiet the panicked passenger. "Tie a rope to him and throw him overboard," Bahlul said. "Just before he drowns, drag him on board. Then he will realize that he is safe on board this ship."[237]

• Catholics and Lutherans can work together, despite past differences. For example, Reverend Vincent Heier, a Catholic in the Archdiocese of St. Louis, invited some Missouri-Kansas Lutherans to meet in St. Louis Cathedral. He welcomed the Lutherans by saying, "We are pleased to provide the cathedral. Please don't nail anything to the doors."[238]

• Joseph Pike and Samuel Randall were asked by Munster Province Meeting to pay visits to several Friends and speak about the subject of plainness. They did an excellent job—before speaking to anyone, they first went through their own homes and got rid of their own superfluities.[239]

Work

• Mulla Nasrudin made plans for the next day, telling his wife, "If it rains, I shall work inside the house, and if it doesn't rain, I shall plow the field." His wife replied, "Whenever you make plans, you should say, 'God willing.'" "Why?" asked Nasrudin. "It shall either rain or not rain. There is no third choice." The next day was sunny, so Nasrudin set out to plow his field, but a group of soldiers kidnapped him, forced him to be their guide to the next town, then beat him for his trouble. Late at night, all black and blue, Nasrudin returned home. His wife had locked the door, so Nasrudin knocked. His wife asked, "Who is it?" Nasrudin replied, "It is I—God willing."[240]

• Zen masters sometimes hide themselves, appearing to be ordinary people while practicing Zen in secret. One such Zen master took an unusual occupation in Japan—he ran a floating outdoor tea room. He searched for spots of natural beauty, filled with flowers and beautiful scents, then made tea there for anyone who wanted it. This sign announced his prices: "The price of tea is however much you give me, from a hundred pounds of gold to half a penny. You can even drink for free, if you like; but I can't give you a better bargain than that."[241]

• Pope John XXIII went out of his way to visit the poor sections of Rome. On one visit, he spoke with a 12-year-old boy and asked what he wanted to be when

---

237. Source: Massud Farzan, *Another Way of Laughter*, p. 83.
238. Source: Cal and Rose Samra, *Holy Humor*, pp. 177-178.
239. Source: William H. Sessions, collector, *Laughter in Quaker Grey*, p. 21.
240. Source: Charles Downing, *Tales of the Hodja*, p. 12.
241. Source: Thomas Cleary, translator, *Zen Antics*, pp. 3-4.

he grew up. The boy answered, "Pope, like you." Pope John XXIII replied, "You've chosen a difficult vocation. It is—you can believe me—a life of sacrifice."[242]

• Joe "Ducky" Medwick, a major league baseball player for the St. Louis Cardinals, met the Pope in the company of several people who announced their occupations: "I'm a comic," "I'm a singer," etc. When it was Ducky's turn to be presented to the Pope, he said, "Your Holiness, I'm a Cardinal."[243]

• At an outdoor rally at which Pope John Paul II spoke, workers were warned against calling the portable potties "Porta-Johns," as the Holy Father might find the name offensive. Therefore, the workers called the portable potties "Vati-Cans."[244]

Yom Kippur

• Although most Jews fast on Yom Kippur, Jews are permitted to eat if they are gravely ill. When the Rabbi of Rachmistrivka became gravely ill, his physician decided that the Rabbi would have to eat on Yom Kippur. The physician was loath to tell the Rabbi this, so he stammered when he spoke to him. The Rabbi listened, then he asked, "What are you trying to say? Are you trying to tell me that I must eat on Yom Kippur?" The physician answered, "Yes." The Rabbi then said, "Important decisions such as that should be clearly stated. In such important matters, you must be completely decisive."[245]

• In 1965, the World Series was played between the Los Angeles Dodgers and the Minneapolis Twins. The opening game of the World Series was on Yom Kippur, and Dodger pitcher Sandy Koufax went to the synagogue rather than the ball park. Fellow Dodger Don Drysdale was on the mound, where he gave up six runs before being taken out of the game in the third inning. After being taken out, Mr. Drysdale told his manager, "I bet right now you wish I was Jewish, too."[246]

• On Yom Kippur, the voice of radio deejay Phil Spector was on the air when a Jewish man telephoned him and asked indignantly, "How can you, a Jewish boy, be working on Yom Kippur?" Mr. Spector replied, "I'm not working—I'm on tape."[247]

---

242. Source: Kurt Klinger, *A Pope Laughs*, p. 64.
243. Source: Michael J. Pellowski, *Baseball's Funniest People*, p. 14.
244. Source: Kate Clinton, *Don't Get Me Started*, p. 152.
245. Source: Shmuel Himelstein, *Words of Wisdom, Words of Wit*, p. 45.
246. Source: Rabbi Joseph Telushkin, *Jewish Wisdom*, p. 509.
247. Source: Bill Adler, *Jewish Wit and Wisdom*, p. 59.

Zen

• Westerners can go to a Zen temple and meditate if they wish, but they must follow the rules, one of which is that they arrive early for meditation. While in Japan, Robert E. Kennedy was meditating at a Zen center when an American Catholic Sister arrived late for meditation. The senior monk stared at her in astonishment, then he picked up his stick—used to hit the meditators when their attention drifts—advanced toward the Sister, raised it above his head, then hit the floor beside the Sister with a loud whack. The Sister began backing away, and again the senior monk raised the stick above his head, then he hit the floor beside the Sister with a loud whack. Now the Sister began running toward the doorway, and the senior monk ran after her and hit the door frame with a loud whack. The purpose of this was not to hurt the Sister, but simply to let her know that one is never tardy for a meditation session. After that demonstration, no one was ever tardy again.[248]

• In the year 1582, some soldiers sought refuge at a Zen temple. When their enemy arrived at the temple and demanded that the soldiers be given to them, the abbot, Kwaisen, refused. Therefore, the enemy locked Kwaisen and the monks under him in a tower, then they set the tower on fire. Inside the tower, Kwaisen gave his final sermon, saying, "For peaceful meditation, we need not go to the mountains and streams. When thoughts are quiet, fire itself is cool and refreshing." Kwaisen and the other monks died without making a sound.[249]

• A student asked Zen master Qianfeng where the road that leads directly to Nirvana is located. Qianfeng used his staff to draw a line in the dirt in front of him, then he said, "The road begins right here."[250]

248. Source: Robert E. Kennedy, *Zen Spirit, Christian Spirit*, p. 56.
249. Source: Sushila Blackman, compiler and editor, *Graceful Exits*, p. 87.
250. Source: Chih-Chung Tsai, *Zen Speaks*, p. 135.

250 Anecdotes About Families

Alcohol

• Comedian Jay Leno doesn't drink, smoke, or use illegal drugs. When Mavis Nicholson, who became his wife, asked for a drink early in their relationship, she almost did not become his wife. He told her, "Look, let me give you the money, and you can buy a blouse or something. I don't want to buy you a drink." With the $35 he gave her, she bought a blouse. (Mavis says, "I can't begin to tell you how absolutely *peculiar* I thought that was.")[1]

• Olivia Pound's father was a Nebraska judge in the 19th century. Once, a lawyer who was also an alcoholic attempted to argue a case before him, even though the lawyer was obviously inebriated. The judge listened for a few minutes, then banged his gavel and ruled, "This case is postponed for two weeks. The lawyer is trying to practice before two bars at the same time. It can't be done."[2]

Animals

• When Darci Kistler, a ballerina for the New York City Ballet, was growing up, her family had a pet alligator named Iggy. One day, Iggy got loose and made his way into the family swimming pool, where the family had a terrible time trying to catch him. Every time a family member tried to catch Iggy with a net, Iggy crushed the net in his jaws. Darci was relieved when Iggy was finally captured and returned to the pet store—she had noticed Iggy eying the family's dog and cat in a suspiciously hungry manner. Other family pets included snakes—once a boa constrictor was loose in the Kistler family house for a week.[3]

• On his TV show *House Party*, Art Linkletter interviewed a little girl whose fish had recently died. He asked whether the fish had gone to fish heaven, but the little girl replied, "No, I threw him down the toilet."[4]

---

1. Source: Bill Adler and Bruce Cassiday, *The World of Jay Leno: His Humor and His Life*, p. 109.
2. Source: Helen White Charles, collector and editor, *Quaker Chuckles*, p. 25.
3. Source: Darci Kistler, *Ballerina: My Story*, p. 16.

Automobiles

• As a child, future Secretary of State Madeleine Albright traveled with her family as they moved to Denver, Colorado—a city that is known as the "Mile-High City" because it is one mile above sea level. Approaching the city, young Madeleine waited for the road to steeply climb one mile skyward, not realizing that the car had been gradually climbing higher for a long time.[5]

• Comedian Jay Leno really, really likes cars and motorcycles. In fact, his garage looks like a warehouse because it is so filled with his vehicular possessions. Still, whenever his mother visited him and wanted to borrow a car, he would tell her, "Mother, I'll *rent* you a car."[6]

Birth

• When Erma Bombeck's first book, *At Wit's End*, was published, she went on tour to publicize it. At one book signing, she spent three hours in a department store with a stack of her books on the desk at which she was sitting, but only two people approached her: A woman wanted directions to the ladies room, and a man asked her the price of the desk. Later, after she had written several best sellers, the lines of people waiting to have her autograph a book became very long. Once, a woman with an infant waited in line to have Ms. Bombeck sign a book. When Ms. Bombeck said that the infant was adorable, the woman replied, "Thank you. It was born in the line."[7]

• When comedian Henry Morgan was five years old, he was taken to a hospital where his mother was having a baby. He walked into her room, pointed to her stomach, and said, "I can see the baby." However, his mother smiled and said, "I've already had the baby." In his autobiography, Mr. Morgan writes, "This gift of saying the right thing at the right time has been with me all my life."[8]

• Entertainer Art Linkletter's daughter, Sharon, was giving birth. Because her physician knew her only by her married name, he was shocked when Mr. Linkletter showed up at the hospital. He told Sharon, "Guess who's waiting to see you on the other side of those doors—Art Linkletter!" Sharon shocked him further by saying, "Why shouldn't he be here? He's my father."[9]

4.   Source: Kermit Schafer, *Best of Bloopers*, p. 42.
5.   Source: Megan Howard, *Madeleine Albright*, p. 35.
6.   Source: Bill Adler and Bruce Cassiday, *The World of Jay Leno: His Humor and His Life*, p. 6.
7.   Source: Susan Edwards, *Erma Bombeck*, p. 160.
8.   Source: Henry Morgan, *Here's Morgan!*, pp. 64-65.

• The most comedian Eddie Cantor ever laughed was in response to a line by Amanda, his four-year-old granddaughter. Mr. Cantor was in the hospital for minor surgery, and Amanda was allowed to see him as long as she was a good girl. At the end of the visit, Amanda asked, "Wasn't I a good girl, Grandpa?" Then she added, "So now may I see the baby?"[10]

• While Eve Arden, famous especially for her radio and TV lead character in *Our Miss Brooks*, was having labor pains for her son, Douglas, she ran into one small problem—nurses in the pre-labor room kept asking her for her autograph.[11]

Birthdays

• Carmine Buete was a 10-year-old boy with AIDS who lived near New York City. He caught AIDS from his mother, who died when he was a year and three months old—he was so young when his mother died that he couldn't remember her. Still, whenever the wind blew open the door of his home, he would say that it was his mother. On his mother's birthday, he used to send her a helium-filled balloon by standing on a porch, releasing the balloon, and letting it soar into the sky. After Carmine died on July 13, 1996, his family started sending balloons to him on his birthday.[12]

• Comedian and announcer Henry Morgan is married to an intelligent woman. On one of his birthdays, an old friend of Henry's called him on the telephone to talk over old times. Throughout the rest of the day at half-hour intervals, more old friends of Henry's kept calling him. He found out later that his wife, Karen, had spent a week tracking down his old friends and assigning them a time to call.[13]

• Humorist Frank Sullivan enjoyed birthdays very much, but he enjoyed even more making jokes at his friends' expense. A friend who sent him a congratulatory telegram sometimes received a telegram like this in reply: "Your telegram on my birthday today will suffice until you can find time to send me some more substantial gift. Thanking you in advance, Mr. Sullivan."[14]

9.   Source: Art Linkletter, *I Didn't Do It Alone*, p. 88.
10.   Source: Eddie Cantor, *The Way I See It*, p. 192.
11.   Source: Eve Arden, *Three Phases of Eve*, p. 97.
12.   Source: Arlene Schulman, *Carmine's Story*, pp. 5, 31, 33.
13.   Source: Henry Morgan, *Here's Morgan!*, p. 295.
14.   Source: J. Bryan III, *Merry Gentlemen (and One Lady)*, p. 83.

Books

• An 8th grade student didn't read a book for her book report, but instead made up a book and completely invented the plot and characters while telling her teacher that she had bought the book at a bookstore and had left it at home and therefore couldn't remember such things as its publisher and copyright. The student received a good grade on the book report, but the teacher wrote a note on her report, asking where he could buy a copy of the book as a present for his niece. The student was so unnerved by the teacher's note that she never cheated again.[15]

• Reading can educate people. Author Walter Dean Myers once received a letter from a teenager who had been watching television coverage of the Persian Gulf War and was so excited that he could hardly wait to turn 17 so he could join the Army and fight in a war. However, after reading Mr. Myers' realistic war book, *Fallen Angels*, he decided that he did not want to fight after all. *Fallen Angels* was a tribute to Mr. Myers' younger brother, Sonny, who died two days after being sent to Vietnam.[16]

• Author Judy Blume loved books even when she was a little girl. In fact, she loved the picture book *Madeline* so much that after borrowing it from a library, she didn't want to return it. Instead, she hid the book and then told her mother that she had lost it.[17]

Brothers

• Two brothers, one of whom was married and the other single, farmed the same land together, and they split the harvest equally. The brother who was single felt that the brother who was married should have more of the harvest, so he would secretly take sacks of grain from his storehouse and put them in the married brother's storehouse. However, the brother who was married worried that the brother who was single was lonely, and in order to allow his brother to buy nice things for himself, he would secretly take sacks of grain from his storehouse and put them in the single brother's storehouse. Year after year, both brothers received an equal number of sacks of grain, and neither understood why.[18]

---

15. Source: Arthur Blumberg and Phyllis Blumberg, *The Unwritten Curriculum*, pp. 108-109.
16. Source: Denise M. Jordan, *Walter Dean Myers: Writer for Real Teens*, pp. 82, 89-90.
17. Source: Christine M. Hill, *Ten Terrific Authors for Teens*, p. 10.
18. Source: James Fadiman and Robert Frager, *Essential Sufism*, p. 186.

• When he was growing up, Cordell Brown and his brother Phil played their own version of dodge ball—instead of throwing a ball, Phil threw very ripe peaches at Cordell. Because Cordell had cerebral palsy, he seldom got out of the way of the peaches, so he became a mess very quickly. Today, they laugh when they recall those games. (Cordell is a wonderful man who has founded a summer camp called Camp Echoing Hills and several residential homes for handicapped adults in Ohio.)[19]

• At a trial, the prosecutor tried to get Wilson Mizner to admit that he was covering up in order to save his brother, Addison. The prosecutor asked Wilson, who was on the witness stand, "You love your brother, don't you? You have a great affection for him, don't you?" Unfortunately for the prosecutor, Wilson had lots of experience on the witness stand. He replied, "I have a vague regard for him."[20]

Chanukah

• On Chanukah, parents customarily give gifts, such as coins, to their children. One Chanukah, actor Elliott Gould told his children, "Tonight, instead of money, I'm going to give you total honesty and truth, which is more important." His daughter, Molly, replied, "But you give us that every night."[21]

Children

• Maud Gruss was born into a French circus family, and at age three, she decided to make an unscheduled public appearance in a balancing act. A cousin named Eddy Ringenbach was performing with his sister, Isabelle, and with Maud's brother, Armand. Eddy was lying on his back, using his legs to support a ladder, on which Isabelle and Armand were performing tricks. Suddenly, young Maud walked out, dressed in a pink tutu, climbed over Eddy, and started to climb up the ladder. The circus audience started to applaud, and Maud, hearing the applause, let go of the ladder and started to applaud, too. As she applauded, she began to fall. Isabelle and Armand immediately jumped off the ladder. Isabelle did a back flip, and Armand did a front flip. When Armand landed, he was holding Maud safely in his arms. The circus audience thought they had witnessed

---

19. Source: Cordell Brown, *I am What I am by the Grace of God*, p. 33.
20. Source: John Burke, *Rogue's Progress: The Fabulous Adventures of Wilson Mizner*, p. 245.
21. Source: Tim Boxer, *The Jewish Celebrity Hall of Fame*, p. 127.

a perfectly performed, much-rehearsed trick, and they gave three-year-old Maud and the other performers an enormous ovation.[22]

• When world-class women's gymnastics coaches Bela and Marta Karolyi defected from Romania to the United States, they did not know English and had a difficult time learning it. When they brought their young daughter, Andrea, to the United States, she also did not know English, and they were worried about her. They tried a public school and a private school, but at both schools the teachers did not pay particular attention to Andrea, who sat silently. Eventually, however, Andrea picked up English on her own. Bela saw her speaking to some American kids, and he asked if she was speaking Romanian or Hungarian to them. Andrea replied, "I'm talking like everybody else." After that experience, Bela and Marta decided that "the best teachers were the children."[23]

• Operatic tenor Leo Slezak knew how to get the truth from his children when they were small—all he had to do was to tell them that he would ask the Angel what had happened and the Angel would tell him. Once, his young son, Walter, refused to eat his supper. He put the food in his mouth, but he would not swallow it. Once he left the room for a moment, returned, and said with a big grin, "I've eaten it now!" Mr. Slezak was doubtful, so he said that he would ask the Angel. Feeling cocky, Walter told him to go ahead and do just that. Mr. Slezak then said that the Angel had told him that Walter had given his food to the family dog, and Walter turned pale and stammered, "How could the Angel find that out?"[24]

• While the Three Stooges were performing live on stage, Sandy, the five-year-old niece of Larry Fine—the balding but not bald Stooge—was in the audience, watching as the Stooges slapped each other and poked each other's eyes. However, at one point, when Moe led a screaming Larry around the stage after sticking his finger up Larry's nose, Sandy started yelling, "You're hurting my Uncle Larry! You're hurting my Uncle Larry!" Larry immediately came over to her and explained that he was only pretending to be hurt, then he rejoined the act to the loud applause of the audience. As for Moe, he was laughing so hard that it took a while for the act to continue.[25]

• Horror writer Anne Rice got her first name from an unusual source: herself. Her name at birth was Howard Allen O'Brien. This name is unusual in itself, and she was given it in part because her father, Howard, had been bullied at school

22.   Source: Alain Chenevière, *Maud in France*, pp. 4-7.
23.   Source: Bela Karolyi and Nancy Ann Richardson, *Feel No Fear*, pp. 127-128.
24.   Source: Leo Slezak, *Song of Motley*, pp. 127-128.
25.   Source: Morris "Moe" Feinberg, *Larry: The Stooge in the Middle*, pp. 142-143.

because some other children thought "Howard" sounded like a girl's name. On the first day young Howard started attending Redemptorist School in New Orleans, a nun asked her for her name. Young Howard replied, "It's Anne!" This name turned out to be OK with her mother, who said, "If she wants to be Anne, it's Anne." Anne received the rest of her adult name after she married Stan Rice.[26]

• Early in her gymnastics career, when she was still a pre-teen, Shannon Miller attended a meet in Las Vegas, and she stayed at the Circus Circus Hotel. When she returned home, she had a lot of stuffed animals with her. Her mother asked where she had gotten them, and young Shannon joked, "Gambling." The real story was that a man in the hotel had asked if she liked stuffed animals. She had replied, "Sure," and he had given her a bunch of stuffed animals he had just won. (Her parents did talk to her about not accepting gifts from strangers.)[27]

• While making a personal appearance in Chicago, TV's Mister Rogers asked if anyone in the audience had anything they wanted to share. A small boy spoke up: "Mister Rogers, I just wear diapers at night now." Of course, the audience wondered how Mister Rogers would react to this sharing. He replied to the boy, "Well, that's very important, and it's up to you when you'll give up your diapers at night. I'm really proud of the ways you're growing." This made the small boy very happy and the audience breathed a sigh of relief at Mister Rogers' answer.[28]

• Frank Bunker Gilbreth raised a dozen children in the early 20th century. With such a large brood, he wasn't above getting a break on expenses now and then. Whenever he came to a toll road, he would look at the toll keeper, identify his nationality, then say, using the appropriate accent, "Do my Irishmen [or Dutchmen, or Scotsmen] come cheaper by the dozen?" Often, the reply would come back, "Irishmen, is it? And I might have known it….The Lord Jesus didn't mean for any family like that to pay toll on my road. Drive through on the house."[29]

• As a child athlete, Robin Campbell competed in many national and international track and field events, necessitating absences from home. During one long absence, she rejoiced that she had gotten out of doing the dishes, which she did each Monday when she was home. However, her family believed that children should do chores, so when Robin returned home, she discovered that she had

---

26.   Source: Bob Madison, *American Horror Writers*, pp. 73, 75-76.
27.   Source: Claudia Miller, *Shannon Miller: My Child, My Hero*, p. 34.
28.   Source: Fred Rogers, *You Are Special*, p. 40.
29.   Source: Frank B. Gilbreth, Jr., and Ernestine Gilbreth Carey, *Cheaper by the Dozen*, p. 22.

been scheduled to wash dishes for a whole week so she could catch up to the work done by her siblings while she was away.[30]

• Chase, the young son of Christian writer Dale Hanson Bourke, had a babysitter who had lost a leg when she was a young girl in Peru, leaving her with a wooden leg which caused her to limp. One day, Ms. Bourke saw the babysitter and young Chase walking together, and she noticed that her son was limping before he came running to her. The babysitter, Doris, explained, "He always walks that way with me." When Ms. Bourke asked why, Doris replied, "So we can be alike."[31]

• While on his own as a youngster after running away from home, comedian W.C. Fields would sometimes crawl through a punched-out window into a cellar where he would sleep by a furnace. This was very good quarters for him at that time. Unfortunately, one day he discovered that the window had been fixed, probably because he had been stealing the housewife's preserves. "The thing taught me a lesson," he said later. "You've got to know where to stop."[32]

• When he was a 12-year-old boy living in New Concord, Ohio, astronaut John Glenn wanted to be a Boy Scout, but there was no local troop for him to join. No problem. He and his friends organized their own scouting group and called it the Ohio Rangers. They engaged in such activities as swimming upstream, hiking in snow, and sleeping outdoors in the rain. Mr. Glenn says, "We told one another we were tougher than Scouts—so tough they wouldn't have us."[33]

• Lady Astor, the first woman to sit in either of the British Houses of Parliament, was once heckled by a woman who shouted, "My children are as good as yours." Lady Astor replied, "As which of mine? I've got some worse than any of yours—but I might have one who is better." Another time, a man shouted, "Your husband's a millionaire, ain't he?" Lady Astor replied, "I should certainly hope so—that's why I married him."[34]

• The two young sons of Francis Hodgson Burnett, author of *A Little Princess* and *The Secret Garden*, supported James Garfield during his Presidential election. The boys used to hang from one of their upstairs windows and shout, "Rah for Garfield!" After he was elected, they were invited to the White House, where they rode their bicycles in the halls and knocked down Senators and other VIPs.[35]

---

30.   Source: Diana C. Gleasner, *Track and Field*, p. 44.
31.   Source: Dale Hanson Bourke, *Everyday Miracles*, pp. 55-56.
32.   Source: Robert Lewis Taylor, *W.C. Fields: His Follies and Fortunes*, p. 23.
33.   Source: Barbara Kramer, *John Glenn: A Space Biography*, p. 12.
34.   Source: Kenneth Williams, *Acid Drops*, p. 47.

• When R' Dov Ber of Mezritch was an eight-year-old boy, the home of his family burned down. His mother began to cry, and so he asked why she was crying. She replied that it wasn't because of the house, but because the fire had destroyed a document recording the family tree, which went back to R' Yochanan HaSandlar. The child replied, "Don't worry, mother. I will be the start of a new family tree."[36]

• Groucho Marx' young daughter, Melinda, came to him one night and asked him to tell her the bedtime story "Little Red Riding Hood." Because Groucho was busy, he asked her if someone else could tell the story to her. But Melinda insisted that he told the story better than anyone else. When Groucho asked why, she explained, "Because you put more food in Red Riding Hood's basket."[37]

• Comedian Joe E. Brown was loved by children. He tells about a letter written by one of the mothers of those children. Just six years old, the child saw one of Mr. Brown's movies, then asked his mother, "Mommy, when Joe E. Brown dies, will he go to Heaven?" The child's mother replied, "Why, of course, darling." "Golly, Mommy," the child said. "Won't God laugh!"[38]

• A friend of author Sharon Salzberg had a four-year-old son whose caregiver, to whom he was very attached, was going to move away to live with her sister and so would not be able to take care of him any more. She explained this carefully to him, and he said, "Mommy, tell me that story again but with a different ending."[39]

• On the First Sunday in Lent, the pastor visited a Sunday School class taught by Rolf E. Aaseng. The pastor wore his clerical vestments and spoke about why the vestments' colors change during the year. One little girl was very impressed and later told her mother, "God came to Sunday School today!"[40]

• A church-going young mother and her two young daughters were shopping in a health-food store when a tall, strong, white-robe-wearing elderly man with long, white hair and beard walked in. The younger daughter stared at the man until her older sister told her, "No, Regan, it's not God."[41]

35. Source: Angelica Shirley Carpenter and Jean Shirley, *Frances Hodgson Burnett: Beyond the Secret Garden*, p. 46.

36. Source: Shmuel Himelstein, *A Touch of Wisdom, A Touch of Wit*, p. 235.

37. Source: Arthur Marx, *Life With Groucho*, p. 296.

38. Source: Joe E. Brown, *Laughter is a Wonderful Thing*, p. 214.

39. Source: Sharon Salzberg, *A Heart as Wide as the World*, pp. 102-103.

40. Source: Rolf E. Aaseng, *Anyone Can Teach (they said)*, p. 63.

41. Source: Ken Alley, *Awkward Christian Soldiers*, pp. 49-50.

• The Reverend James Bence was visiting the family of the Reverend Ed Crandall when he asked Crandall's young son, "Well, Steve, have you been a good boy lately?" Steve answered, "Yes." The Reverend Bence then asked, "Are you good all of the time?" Young Steve answered, "Well, are *you*?"[42]

• A prosthesis (an artificial limb) is a useful thing, but it can cause some strange phone calls. A mother once received this call from a camp for children with cancer: "Mrs. Anderson? Robin broke a leg on the trail. Could you please send up another one on a plane?"[43]

• English entertainer Joyce Grenfell had an Uncle Buck who was a rolling stone. According to family lore, when his youngest child was being taught the prayer, "Our father which art in Heaven," the child looked up and said, "Mama, where's Papa gone now?"[44]

• Art Linkletter used to interview very young children, and he had great success asking them what their parents had told them not to say on the show. A little girl once responded, "She told me not to announce that she was pregnant."[45]

• As a child, violinist Mischa Elman played Beethoven's *Kreutzer Sonata*, which includes some long pauses, before some relatives. During one of the pauses, his aunt asked, "Why don't you play something you know, Mischa?"[46]

• As a child, Frida Kahlo was mischievous. Sometimes, she soaped the steps near where Mexican artist Diego Rivera was working, in the hope that he would slip on the stairs and fall. When she grew up, she married Mr. Rivera.[47]

• Country comedian Jerry Clower has children who can make him laugh. When his daughter, Katy Burns, was four, she pulled off her gloves, then called, "Daddy! Daddy! If I had one more finger, I could count to 11."[48]

• Ballerina Anna Pavlova was made very happy when she received a copy of a child's essay that began, "Once I saw a fairy. Her name was Anna Pavlova."[49]

---

42. Source: William Woughter, *All Preachers of Our God & King*, p. 10.
43. Source: Erma Bombeck, *I Want to Grow Hair, I Want to Grow Up, I Want to Go to Boise*, p. 116.
44. Source: Joyce Grenfell, *Joyce Grenfell Requests the Pleasure*, p. 12.
45. Source: Kermit Schafer, *All Time Great Bloopers*, p. 20.
46. Source: David Ewen, *Listen to the Mocking Words*, p. 40.
47. Source: Doreen Gonzales, *Diego Rivera: His Art, His Life*, p. 64.
48. Source: Jerry Clower, *Life Everlaughter*, p. 66.
49. Source: A.H. Franks, editor, *Pavlova: A Collection of Memoirs*, p. 44.

Christmas

• Early in the 20th century, a custom in some parts of the United States was to tie presents to a Christmas tree at the church and have Santa Claus come to the church for a party and pass out all the presents. At one such Christmas Eve party, a little girl, the daughter of the richest and most miserly man in town, showed up for the party and the passing out of presents. (Her older brothers stayed away because they realized that their father was too stingy to put a present on the tree for them.) As the evening passed, the little girl's name wasn't called even once. Fortunately, Alyene Porter, the youngest daughter of the preacher, noticed what was happening. She told her mother, who re-wrapped Alyene's present to her, a bottle of perfume, and put the little girl's name on it, then surreptitiously hung it on the tree. When Santa Claus finally called her name, the little girl cried out, "He did call it! He did call it! I did get a present!"[50]

• Christmases when religious writer Dale Hanson Bourke was a little girl were sometimes surprising. One Christmas the presents were placed in the shower stall. Her father explained that since their house didn't have a fireplace, Santa Claus must have squeezed through the water pipes to come inside and leave presents. On one Christmas Eve, little Dale was allowed to choose one present to open, so she chose the biggest present. However, her parents had guessed that she would choose that present so they had filled it with nuts. Although everyone laughed, her parents knew that she was disappointed, so they let her open the rest of her presents.[51]

• One Christmas, Pope John XXIII went to a children's hospital to visit the patients. One child, Silvio Colagrande, had been blind, but could now see because a dying priest, Don Gnocchi, had willed his eyes to Silvio and the corneas had been transplanted. Upon seeing the Pope, Silvio called out, "I see you with Don Gnocchi's eyes." Another child, seven-year-old Carmine Gemma, had recently become blind as the result of an attack of meningitis. He told Pope John XXIII, "You're the Pope, I know, but I can't see you." The Pope held Carmine's hands for a while, then he murmured, "We are all blind, sometimes."[52]

• When poet Nikki Giovanni was a small child, her parents, Gus and Yolande, didn't always have the money necessary to buy what their two young daughters wanted. One Christmas, their two daughters wanted bicycles, but Mr. and Mrs. Giovanni could afford to buy them only roller skates. However, they did figure

50.   Source: Alyene Porter, *Papa Was a Preacher*, pp. 146-147.
51.   Source: Dale Hanson Bourke, *Everyday Miracles*, pp. 34-35.
52.   Source: Kurt Klinger, *A Pope Laughs*, pp. 20-21.

out a way to make them happier about not getting bicycles although other children in the neighborhood had. They told her, "Isn't it terrible that their parents gave them bicycles when it's so cold? They won't be able to ride until spring."[53]

• When Leo Slezak's son, Walter, was eight years old, he wrote out a list of presents for Santa Claus to bring to him. However, the governess mentioned to Mr. Slezak that Walter didn't believe in Santa Claus any more. When Mr. Slezak asked Walter why he had written out a list of presents for Santa Claus, little Walter replied, "I didn't want to spoil the pleasure for you and Mommy."[54]

• On Christmas, Pope John XXIII (who was named Angelo Giuseppe Roncalli at his birth) sometimes visited children in a hospital. He once asked a boy what his name was. The boy replied, "Giuseppe." Not knowing who his visitor was, the boy asked, "What's your name?" The Pope answered, "Oh, my name is Giuseppe, too, but now everybody calls me John."[55]

Couples

• In 1994, ice dancers Irina Lobacheva and Ilia Averbukh competed at the World Championships, finishing a respectable 13th. However, the next year this married couple had trouble finding enough food to eat and enough training time in their native Russia and so finished 15th at the 1995 World Championships. Therefore, they moved to Delaware in the United States where they found plenty of food and training time, enabling them to finish 6th at the 1996 World Championships. They kept improving and finally got on the medals stand by finishing third at the 2001 World Championships.[56]

• In the old days, William Boake wished to court Euphemia Birkett, but her guardian, Catherine Tew, disliked him. One day, Mr. Boake arrived to visit Ms. Birkett, but Ms. Tew made sure that her charge was upstairs and out of sight. Mr. Boake was not to be trifled with, so he ran upstairs, and Ms. Tew tried to stop him by grabbing one of the tails of his coat, only to have the tail tear off in her hand. After he and Ms. Birkett were married, Mr. Boake kept the one-tailed coat as a souvenir of his courtship.[57]

• When Jack Gilford was courting Madeline Lee, he was working at a resort and called her long distance. The telephone operator at the resort listened to all

53.   Source: Judith Pinkerton Josephson, *Nikki Giovanni: Poet of the People*, p. 21.

54.   Source: Leo Slezak, *Song of Motley*, pp. 129-130.

55.   Source: Louis Michaels, *The Humor and Warmth of Pope John XXIII*, pp. 10-11.

56.   Source: Gérard Châtaigneau and Steve Milton, *Figure Skating Now: Olympic and World Stars*, p. 115.

57.   Source: William H. Sessions, collector, *More Quaker Laughter*, p. 31.

their conversations and found them very entertaining. Once, after a conversation more than usually filled with passion and drama, Mr. Gilford asked the telephone operator, "How much do I owe you?" With a sob in her throat, the telephone operator said, "Never mind. There's no charge tonight."[58]

• A missionary couple stayed at the home of an elderly widow. When they went to bed, they discovered that the bedding was very wrinkled and very dirty, but they slept in the bed anyway. The next morning, the widow explained, "For years there have been so many holy people who have slept in that bed that I've never been able to change it."[59]

• Track superstar Mary Decker frequently wrote an early boyfriend when she was away from him. While in New York, she wrote him four letters in two days and then telephoned him on the third day—she hadn't received a letter from him yet, and she was worried that something had happened to him.[60]

• A friend of lesbian comedian Judy Carter wore a wedding ring to work. When her co-workers asked what her husband did, she replied, "*She* works for a pharmacy."[61]

Daughters

• Rabbi Joseph Telushkin once watched his two daughters playing together nicely, and he commented to a friend named Dennis Prager how much pleasure this sight was giving him. Mr. Prager asked, "Doesn't it give you more pleasure than if one of your daughters said 'I love you, Daddy' but didn't act nicely to her sister?" Rabbi Telushkin answered, "Of course." Mr. Prager then said, "I imagine God is the same way. He derives greater pleasure when people are good to each other than when they are 'good' to Him but not to each other."[62]

• When Bob Dole's daughter, Robin, was young, she was a great fan of a British rock band, so Senator Dole wrote the British embassy to find out if the band could play at his daughter's high school as a surprise. Unfortunately, he received a reply saying that the Beatles would be too busy to oblige during their first American tour.[63]

• Comic actor Robert Morley once embarrassed his daughter by attempting to surf in Hawaii—he was unable even to mount the surfboard. When his mortified

58.   Source: Kate Mostel and Madeline Gilford, *170 Years of Show Business*, pp. 77-78.
59.   Source: William Woughter, *All Preachers of Our God & King*, pp. 85-86.
60.   Source: Linda Jacobs, *Mary Decker: Speed Records and Spaghetti*, pp. 26, 28.
61.   Source: Judy Carter, *The Homo Handbook*, p. 177.
62.   Source: Rabbi Joseph Telushkin, *Jewish Wisdom*, pp. 175-176.
63.   Source: Bob Dole, *Great Political Wit*, p. 30.

daughter told him, "People were laughing at you," he was unperturbed and replied, "Usually they have to pay to laugh at me."[64]

Death

• Ann Weeks of Lexington, Kentucky, suffered the loss of her husband. Unfortunately, for weeks following the funeral, there were telephone calls from people asking for her husband because they were unaware that he had died. Once, a salesman called and asked for him. Ms. Weeks replied, "I'm sorry, Paul is deceased. I'm his wife. May I help you?" The salesman didn't say anything about her husband's death, but he did tell Ms. Weeks that he was with the Appliance Warranty Center and was calling to remind her that a warranty on an appliance had run out and she needed to renew it. Ms. Weeks replied that she had decided not to renew that warranty. The salesman, annoyed, said, "Well, I'm sure your dead husband would want you to renew." Not liking to be manipulated, Ms. Weeks replied, "Funny you should mention it, but just hours before Paul died he said, 'Honey, whatever you do, don't renew the appliance warranty!'" The salesman hung up.[65]

• Near the end of his life, Al Capp, creator of *Li'l Abner*, was confined to a wheelchair. One day he asked his wife if she had any silver candlesticks and plain white candles in the house. She did, so he asked, "Would you light those candles and put them on the mantelpiece. Tonight, I mean. This is Friday, isn't it, Catherine?" It was Friday, and Catherine did as her husband requested. Later, Al's brother, Elliott Caplin, explained the significance of the candles. In their family, the person who most revered the Sabbath and lit the candles and said the prayers had been their mother. As Al Capp sat in his apartment, knowing that he was dying, he was thinking about his mother.[66]

• Comedian Beatrice Lillie once visited her mother's grave and saw that a small, freshly dug grave was nearby. Filled with pity at the death of an infant, she spent a few weeks tending the grave and planting flowers—originally intended for her own mother's grave—all around it. Later, a friend asked her if she was still tending the grave. She replied that she had discovered that it was the grave of an 85-year-old man, so "I dug up every goddamn plant and put them back on my mother's grave."[67]

---

64. Source: Robert Morley, *Around the World in Eighty-One Years*, p. 46.
65. Source: Cal and Rose Samra, *More Holy Hilarity*, pp. 145-146.
66. Source: Elliott Caplin, *Al Capp Remembered*, pp. 19-20.
67. Source: Bruce Laffey, *Beatrice Lillie*, p. 237.

• Philosopher Richard Watson's father knew that he was dying of cancer. He told his son, "I'm dying. Don't give me any of that crap I'm not." His son replied, "OK, so you're dying. Now what?" In reply, he just grinned. Just before he died, one of his favorite nieces and her husband visited him. At the end of their visit, the husband said, "I want you to be sitting up in a chair next time I see you." He replied, "You don't see too many people buried sitting up."[68]

• A man once drew up a will in which he left everything to his wife and three sons. He then asked the Chafetz Chaim to look over the will and criticize it. After looking over the will, the Chafetz Chaim pointed out that the man had overlooked an important beneficiary: his soul. The will made no provision for charity, and the man's soul deserved to be considered in the will.[69]

• At a funeral, brightly colored clothing is regarded as inappropriate, but not even family members are required to wear black, although many do. Etiquette expert Grace Fox knows a woman who wore a lovely blue dress at the funeral of her husband and touchingly explained that it was her husband's favorite dress.[70]

• After her grandmother died, track superstar Mary Decker ran a race on an indoor track in Los Angeles. She cried the entire distance and finished last.[71]

• In his will, comedian Jack Benny made the provision that his wife, Mary Livingston, be given a perfect red rose every day for the rest of her life.[72]

Easter

• As a teenager, Connie, the daughter of the Rev. Frederick L. Haynes, liked sunrise Easter services even more than Christmas. Now a mother with three sons, each Easter she drags her sons out of bed before sunrise to get ready for the sunrise service. Sometimes they ask her, "Why, Mom?" She replies, "We are Easter people."[73]

Education

• When Ralph Bunche was very young, his mother told him, "My boy, don't ever let anything take away your hope and faith and dreams." After his mother died, Ralph attended high school, but despite high grades, he was kept out of the

---

68.   Source: Richard Watson, *The Philosopher's Diet*, p. 147.
69.   Source: Shmuel Himelstein, *Words of Wisdom, Words of Wit*, p. 166.
70.   Source: Grace Fox, *Everyday Etiquette*, p. 270.
71.   Source: Linda Jacobs, *Mary Decker: Speed Records and Spaghetti*, pp. 37-38.
72.   Source: Henny Youngman, *Take My Life, Please!*, p. 207.
73.   Source: Cal and Rose Samra, *More Holy Hilarity*, p. 185.

city-wide honor society known as the Ephebian Society simply because he was black. He thought about quitting school, but then he remembered what his mother had told him and so he stayed in school. In 1922, he became valedictorian of his high school. In 1934, he earned a Ph.D. in political science and international relations from Harvard University. In 1950, because of his work with the United Nations, he became the first African American to win the Nobel Peace Prize.[74]

• World-class women's gymnastics coach Bela Karolyi was born in communist Romania and so after he defected to the United States he did not know English well. Once, his daughter, Andrea, came home from school and requested help with an assignment: to make a New Year's resolution. Bela was outraged, screaming, "No revolution, no revolution in my house. Absolutely no revolution." His wife, Marta, came home later and asked why Bela wasn't helping their daughter. Bela replied, "Marta, her teacher wants us to help her start a revolution. I won't be a part of that!" Fortunately, his wife was able to explain the homework assignment to him.[75]

• When Angelo Giuseppe Roncalli (who was later to be Pope John XXIII) was a child, he became lazy in his studies, so his parents gave him a letter and sent him to give it to a local priest. Angelo was suspicious about the letter's contents, so he opened it and read it. After reading that the letter told the priest to give him a good scolding for not studying harder, Angelo tore up the letter and threw it away. (Despite not being scolded by the priest, Angelo did thereafter pay more attention to his studies.)[76]

• A young man, the son of a preacher, once attended a Bible college. Coming home for the weekend, he decided to do his Bible study homework while sitting in church as his father preached. Later, his father asked what he had been doing. The young man confessed that he had been doing his homework, and his father asked, "Don't you think you should be listening to the sermon?" Today, the young man says that he is the only person ever to get in trouble for studying the Bible in church.[77]

• Once an elderly couple met the president of Harvard. They told him that they would like to know more about Harvard before making a contribution in memory of their son, who had been killed in war. However, the couple were

---

74. Source: Anne Schraff, *Ralph Bunche: Winner of the Nobel Peace Prize*, pp. 17-18, 21, 115-116.
75. Source: Bela Karolyi and Nancy Ann Richardson, *Feel No Fear*, p. 135.
76. Source: Kurt Klinger, *A Pope Laughs*, p. 17.
77. Source: Ken Alley, *Awkward Christian Soldiers*, pp. 86-87.

plainly dressed and the president of Harvard quickly brushed them off. So the elderly couple went to northern California and used their money to establish Stanford University, in memory of their son, Leland Stanford.[78]

• In 1958, Suzanne Farrell—at that time she was a very young Cincinnati, Ohio, dance student whose real name was Roberta Ficker—learned that the famous New York City Ballet was performing in Bloomington, Indiana. Her mother supported her daughter's dance ambitions, and so she wrote a note to excuse her daughter's absence (because of illness, she wrote) and they took a day off to enjoy the dance performance.[79]

• A little girl went to kindergarten for the first time with her mother walking her the short distance to school. After her mother had left, the little girl needed to go to the bathroom, so her teacher said she could leave the classroom. The little girl then walked home, where she went to the bathroom. Later, the little girl was surprised to learn that there were bathrooms at school, just like there were at home.[80]

• A cat walked into an elementary school classroom, where the young students immediately gathered around it, fed it milk, and tried to guess its sex. A little girl said, "I know how we can tell its sex." Her teacher wasn't especially thrilled to hear this, and she was relieved when the little girl continued, "We can vote on it."[81]

• English schoolboys sometimes make a lot of noise when applauding, including stomping with their feet. Whenever his schoolboys stomped, Frederick Andrews, the headmaster of Ackworth, would tell them, "I like you to applaud with all your hearts, but not with all your soles."[82]

Fathers

• As a teenager, President Bill Clinton's Secretary of State Madeleine Albright went on dates that were not like the typical dates of today's American girls. Although she had moved to the United States as a girl, Ms. Albright was born in Czechoslovakia, and her father followed old-world ideas about dating. He would let Ms. Albright's boyfriend drive her to wherever the date would happen, but he followed them in his own car and went on the date with them. After the date was

78.   Source: Wayne Dosick, *Golden Rules*, pp. 51-52.
79.   Source: Suzanne Farrell, *Holding On to the Air*, pp. 19, 35.
80.   Source: Arthur Blumberg and Phyllis Blumberg, *The Unwritten Curriculum*, pp. 15-17.
81.   Source: Logan Munger Brady, *Amusing Anecdotes*, p. 26.
82.   Source: William H. Sessions, collector, *Laughter in Quaker Grey*, p. 105.

over, he drove his daughter home while her boyfriend followed them in his car, then Mr. Albright invited his daughter's boyfriend in for milk and cookies. Needless to say, Ms. Albright didn't keep boyfriends for long. (Nevertheless, she did get married and gave birth to three daughters.)[83]

• Comedian Albert Brooks' father was funny. In a restaurant, he would sometimes stand up and announce to the other diners, "I want your attention, all of you. This boy [his son Albert] is not eating his vegetables." As a high school student, Albert did an imitation of escape artist Harry Houdini as an incompetent who couldn't even get his hands out of his own pockets. This impressed family friend Carl Reiner so much that when Johnny Carson asked him on *The Tonight Show* who were the funniest people he knew, he named Mel Brooks and young Albert.[84]

• Choreographer Martha Graham's father was a doctor. When she was a child, he showed her a drop of water on a slide and asked what she saw. Of course, she replied that she saw a drop of water. He asked if the water was pure, and she answered that it was. Dr. Graham then asked her to look at it with a microscope. She did, and she saw lots of bacteria in the water. "Yes, it is impure," Dr. Graham said. "Just remember this all your life, Martha. You must look for the truth."[85]

• Just before the short program at the 2001 World Championships, figure skater Michelle Kwan had a problem when the heel of one skate came loose. According to figure skating rules, if you don't have your equipment prepared to skate when your name is called, you are disqualified. Fortunately, Ms. Kwan's father came to the rescue. He fixed the heel by using six screws—and three tubes of super glue. (Yes, Michelle won the gold medal.)[86]

• Kerry Strug's father once told her that she was his least expensive child, because the only gifts she ever wanted were leotards and because she never wore out her shoes since she was always walking on her hands. (Later, Ms. Strug became an elite gymnast and her father had to pay out big bucks for her training—the training paid off with a gold medal at the 1996 Olympics in Atlanta.)[87]

• Olympic gymnast Shannon Miller once performed a very bad vault that sent her crashing to the mat. Her father, Ron, is a university professor who uses video of that vault to teach his class some principles of physics. The agreement Shan-

83. Source: Megan Howard, *Madeleine Albright*, pp. 38-39.
84. Source: Phil Berger, *The Last Laugh*, pp. 238-239.
85. Source: Carin T. Ford, *Legends of American Dance and Choreography*, p. 7.
86. Source: Gérard Châtaigneau and Steve Milton, *Figure Skating Now: Olympic and World Stars*, p. 46.
87. Source: Kerri Strug, *Landing on My Feet*, p. 5.

non and her father made is that after he shows the video of the very bad vault, he has to show a video of her performing the vault flawlessly.[88]

• Cordell Brown has cerebral palsy and two sons. (He also founded a summer camp called Camp Echoing Hills and several residential homes for handicapped adults in Ohio.) He never asked his sons about his disability until they were grown, then he asked if having a father with cerebral palsy had made life difficult for them. They answered, "Dad, you've just always been Dad."[89]

• Gay comedian Bob Smith warned his boyfriend, Tom, that his father, a retired state trooper, judged people by their handshake, so that when they met Tom would know to give him a firm handshake. Bob's father once told him, "Bob, I like all your friends because all the men have very solid handshakes, and come to think of it, all the women do, too."[90]

• A Jewish man heard that his father was ill; however, visiting his father would involve an expensive train journey. Knowing that Jewish law does not require a child to spend money to honor a parent, he asked Rabbi Hayyim of Brisk to make a ruling. Rabbi Hayyim quickly made the ruling: "You are not required to spend the money—walk!"[91]

• Joe Garagiola led a very busy life in broadcasting for a long time. How busy was he? He walked into the door of his house one day, and his wife told their three-year-old daughter, "It's Daddy!" His daughter asked, "What channel?" Mr. Garagiola says, "When your own kids only recognize you when you're on TV, it's time to do some thinking."[92]

• Meredith Willson's father, whose favorite movie actress was Anita Stewart, was as stubborn as only a person from Iowa can be. Mr. Willson's father referred to her as "An-eye-ta," and when Mr. Willson told him that she called herself "An-ee-ta," he replied, "She's mistaken."[93]

• A good father had a bad son who gave him trouble and heartbreak. The son even abandoned God. When the father complained to the founder of Hasidism, the Baal Shem Tov, and asked what he should do, the Baal Shem Tov replied, "Love him more than ever."[94]

---

88.   Source: Claudia Miller, *Shannon Miller: My Child, My Hero*, p. 41.
89.   Source: Cordell Brown, *I am What I am by the Grace of God*, p. 169.
90.   Source: Bob Smith, *Openly Bob*, p. 3.
91.   Source: Rabbi Joseph Telushkin, *Jewish Wisdom*, p. 151.
92.   Source: Joe Garagiola, *It's Anybody's Ballgame*, pp. 225-226.
93.   Source: Meredith Willson, *And There I Stood With My Piccolo*, pp. 73-74.
94.   Source: Lawrence J. Epstein, *A Treasury of Jewish Anecdotes*, p. 22.

• A contestant on the old TV show *Name That Tune* was trying to guess a song that was titled "Christopher Columbus." The host of the show gave her a hint: "If he didn't do what he did, you wouldn't be here today." The contestant answered, "My father."[95]

• Comedian Sam Kinison's father is a preacher. Whenever word of Sam's often wild and crazy lifestyle came back home, his father would tell his congregation, "I've been praying for your children for years. Now it's time for you to pray for one of mine."[96]

Food

• This is a story told by Irving Cramer, the Executive Director of MAZON: A Jewish Response to Hunger. A kindergarten teacher once asked her students how many of them had eaten breakfast that morning. About half had, so the teacher asked those who hadn't eaten, why not. Some didn't eat breakfast because they didn't like what was served or because they had gotten up late, but one child said, "It wasn't my turn." The teacher asked the child to explain, and he said, "There are five kids in my family. But we don't have enough money to buy enough food so that everybody can eat breakfast every day. We take turns eating breakfast, and today, it wasn't my turn."[97]

• When Aung San Suu Kyi was a little girl in Burma, she was afraid of the dark, but she wanted to overcome her fear. Each evening, her mother made hot milk for each of the children to drink, but Suu Kyi didn't like her milk hot, so she would leave it to cool, and later each evening, she would drink the milk alone in the dark. She says, "The first few days my heart would go 'thump, thump, thump,' but after five or six days I got quite used to it." In 1991, she won the Nobel Peace Prize for her efforts to bring freedom to the people of Burma.[98]

• Actor Walter Matthau's mother didn't know to cook. One of the things she didn't know how to cook was meat loaf—which she steamed along with assorted vegetables. One day, Mr. Matthau and Jennie, his nine-year-old daughter, went to her house for dinner. After dinner, Mr. Matthau noticed that Jennie's back pocket had a large wet spot, and he asked her about it. She answered, "Don't tell grandma. Please, don't tell grandma." She had stuffed the meatloaf and steamed vegetables in her back pocket.[99]

95. Source: Kermit Schafer, *Best of Bloopers*, p. 92.
96. Source: Hank Gallo, *Comedy Explosion: A New Generation*, p. 72.
97. Source: Wayne Dosick, *Golden Rules*, pp. 80-81.
98. Source: Whitney Stewart, *Aung San Suu Kyi: Fearless Voice of Burma*, pp. 31-32.

• A large family—with seven children between age 3 to age 13—walked into a restaurant. Because there were so many young children in the family, the waitresses and management were worried that they would be rowdy and disturb the other patrons of the restaurant. However, the children knew their manners and behaved correctly—no yelling, no fighting, no playing. When the family had finished eating, the waitress presented them with their bill—with 10 percent deducted for good behavior![100]

• Comedian Eddie Cantor's daughter, Marilyn, grew up to become a good cook—and a good wit. Once she had several people over for dinner; as she was carrying the entree to the table, she dropped it, and suddenly the floor was awash with shrimps swimming in chili sauce. The guests fell silent, but Marilyn said, "Don't just stand there—dig in!"[101]

• Rolf E. Aaseng was once asked by his wife to make some biscuits. He looked in the open cookbook, found that the recipe was for 48 biscuits, so he made 48 biscuits out of the dough. However, his wife had forgotten to tell him that when she made biscuits she halved the recipe. Fortunately, the family dog enjoyed the extra biscuits.[102]

• As pioneers traveled from east to west across North America in covered wagons, often they had very little change in their diets. One pioneer woman with a sense of humor wrote that about the only change in the diet of her and her family consisted of eating bacon and bread instead of bread and bacon.[103]

• Lydia Parker White, a Quaker, was known for her homemade cookies, and her grandchildren frequently asked her for cookies, something that sometimes upset their parents. Once, her granddaughter visited her and after greeting her, said, "Mama told me not to ask thee for cookies today."[104]

Gays and Lesbians

• When financial writer Andrew Tobias finally came out to his parents, he called his mother on the telephone and told her—many of his gay friends regard this way of coming out as lacking grace. Her first words to him were, "Don't tell your father—promise me." After nearly two years, she gave her son permission to

99. Source: Marilyn Hall and Rabbi Jerome Cutler, *The Celebrity Kosher Cookbook*, p. 101.
100. Source: Norton Mockridge, *A Funny Thing Happened…*, p. 12.
101. Source: Eddie Cantor, *The Way I See It*, p. 138.
102. Source: Rolf E. Aaseng, *Anyone Can Teach (they said)*, pp. 93-94.
103. Source: Brandon Marie Miller, *Buffalo Gals: Women of the Old West*, p. 14.
104. Source: Helen White Charles, collector and editor, *Quaker Chuckles*, p. 58.

tell his father. When he did come out to his father—who wasn't surprised—he also gave him an autobiography about being gay that he had published under a pseudonym. His father stayed up all night and read *The Best Little Boy in the World* twice, and he cried because he hadn't realized that his son was a homosexual and was going through so much pain and so he hadn't been there for him. Both parents accepted their son's homosexuality. At a Thanksgiving dinner, his father met Andrew's significant other, Charles Nolan, and told Andrew that Charles "seems like a very fine young man." His mother joked that she wishes Andrew's older, straight brother could have found someone like Charles to settle down with.[105]

• Edythe Eyde watched some new neighbors move in—two men, no women. Her suspicions aroused, she went over and said, "Hi, welcome. I'm your neighbor across the street. I see you have a couple of cats." She played with the cats, then said, "You're gay, aren't you?" The two men were stunned, but she put them at ease by saying, "Well, so am I! Hi, neighbor!" They became good friends and traded jobs as needed. When the gay men went away on business trips, she took care of their cats, and when she needed a difficult-to-replace light bulb changed, they did it for her.[106]

• When comedian Kate Clinton came out to her family as a lesbian, her brother, Bill, decided to tell his children the news. Over dinner, he told them, and Angela, his eleven-year-old daughter, replied, "Well, duh, Dad. I have only known this my entire life."[107]

• Lesbian comedian Judy Carter says that a good way to come out to your friends is to ask, "Are you friends with any gay people?" If they say that they aren't, reply, "Well, you are now."[108]

Gifts

• Quakers are concerned about social justice and about the just distribution of the good things of this world. Long ago, John Cox, Sr., gave hospitality to people travelling west. One guest took a liking to Mr. Cox' son and made him a boat. John Cox, Jr., had only one other toy—a wagon. However, Mr. Cox told his son that he had to give away either the boat or the wagon, because as long as there

---

105. Source: Andrew Tobias, *The Best Little Boy in the World Grows Up*, pp. 29-31.
106. Source: Zsa Zsa Gershick, *Gay Old Girls*, p. 69.
107. Source: Kate Clinton, *Don't Get Me Started*, p. 27.
108. Source: Judy Carter, *The Homo Handbook*, p. 126.

was one child in the world who did not have a toy, he didn't want his son to have two toys.[109]

• When figure skater Dorothy Hamill was 11 years old—in the days before teenagers got their noses pierced as a fashion statement—her friends gave her 13 pairs of earrings. A competition was coming up, and her parents told her that if she won the competition, she could get both ears pierced. However, if she finished second, she could get only one ear pierced, and if she finished third, she could get only her nose pierced.[110]

• At age 13, R.L. Stine received a heavy-duty typewriter as a bar mitzvah gift—a gift he made much use of. During summer vacations in his high school years, he told his parents that he couldn't get a job because he was too busy writing a novel. His parents never questioned this statement. As an adult, Mr. Stein became the author of the *Fear Street* and *Goosebumps* series.[111]

• When American dance pioneers Ted Shawn and Ruth St. Denis married each other, Ms. St. Denis refused to wear a wedding ring because she regarded it as "a symbol of bondage." Later, because Mr. Shawn felt that at least one of them ought to wear a wedding ring, she bought him one as a first-anniversary gift.[112]

• When Giulio Gatti-Casazza was courting soprano Frances Alda, he gave her a perfect lover's gift—a leather-bound volume of love letters he had written to her.[113]

Grandparents

• When Maud Gruss was 12 years old and about to make her first public appearance as a solo tightrope walker, her mother, whose name was Gipsy, showed her a scrapbook filled with photographs and clippings of her own career as a tightrope walker. In one old black-and-white photograph, Maud recognized herself, but Gipsy turned the page, showed her an even older black-and-white photograph, and asked, "And this one, is that you as well?" The young girls in the photographs, although they looked very much like 12-year-old Maud, turned out to be her grandmother, Violette, and her great-grandmother, Germaine, both of whom had been tightrope walkers. (By the way, Maud's public debut went very well, and her father, Alexis, said, "Tonight, a new star is born.")[114]

109. Source: Irvin C. Poley and Ruth Verlenden Poley, *Friendly Anecdotes*, pp. 118-119.
110. Source: William R. Sanford and Carl R. Green, *Dorothy Hamill*, p. 14.
111. Source: Christine M. Hill, *Ten Terrific Authors for Teens*, p. 94.
112. Source: Ted Shawn, *One Thousand and One Night Stands*, pp. 44, 49-50.
113. Source: Frances Alda, *Men, Women, and Tenors*, pp. 103-104.
114. Source: Alain Chenevière, *Maud in France*, pp. 17, 20-21, 24.

• George Beatty was a jewelry maker in Cleveland, Ohio. He once received a letter from a wealthy man who wanted him to create a piece of jewelry for the wealthy man's dearest granddaughter. Mr. Beatty noticed that the letter referred to the granddaughter as "dearest" five times, and he prayed to God for inspiration—a prayer that was answered. He created a ring across which were displayed, in order, a diamond, an emerald, an amethyst, a ruby, another emerald, a sapphire, and a topaz. Why are there two emeralds? Mr. Beatty says, "Because there are two e's in 'dearest.' If you take the initials of those stones, it spells the word 'dearest.'"[115]

• As a child, Russian ice skater Ekaterina Gordeeva used to go mushroom hunting with her grandfather. Because all their neighbors also went mushroom hunting, they tried to get up early so they could find mushrooms before anyone else. However, if they were late, her grandfather would tell her not to worry, because their mushrooms would hide from the other mushroom hunters. According to Ms. Gordeeva, her grandfather was right, because they always found their mushrooms.[116]

• The grandmother of Meredith Willson, author of *The Music Man*, was lying on her deathbed when a truck farmer came by with "triple-strength horseradish guaranteed to grow hair on a china egg." She heard the truck farmer and asked her children to bring her some horseradish and a spoon. She put a spoonful of the horseradish in her mouth, swallowed, then said, "Now there's something with a little character!"[117]

• Fred Rogers, aka Mister Rogers, is named for his grandfather: Fred Brooks McFeely. While Mister Rogers was growing up, his grandfather frequently told him, "I like you, just the way you are." Of course, this is a quotation that he has shared with generations of children who watch his TV show, *Mister Rogers' Neighborhood*.[118]

• One day when he was young, Maury Maverick, Jr., was kissing a girl on his grandmother's front porch, when his grandmother told him to stop that. He replied, "Oh, Grandma, you used to do the same thing back in Virginia behind shutters." His grandmother hit him, then said, "What do you think shutters are for, you young fool?"[119]

115. Source: Donald Grey Barnhouse, *Let Me Illustrate*, pp. 34-35.
116. Source: Ekaterina Gordeeva, *My Sergei*, p. 22.
117. Source: Meredith Willson, *And There I Stood With My Piccolo*, p. 75.
118. Source: Fred Rogers, *You Are Special*, p. xii.
119. Source: Maury Maverick, Jr., *Texas Iconoclast*, pp. 29-30.

• When Ralph Bunche, the first African American to win the Noble Peace Prize, became valedictorian of his high school in 1922, the principal attempted to compliment him to his grandmother by saying that he never thought of Ralph as a Negro. Ralph's grandmother firmly stated, "He is a Negro—and proud of it."[120]

• Frank DeCaro, the author of *A Boy Named Phyllis*, had a grandmother who liked to read trashy novels such as *Valley of the Dolls* and *Airport* while sitting under a hairdryer. Just to keep her family guessing, however, she occasionally varied her reading matter with a book such as *Saints to Know and Love*.[121]

• Jerry Clower's grandson, Jayree, came to visit his grandparents for a while, and his grandmother, Homerline, told him a couple of times to pick up his toys. Jayree ignored her for a while, then he put his hands on his hips and asked Mr. Clower, "Grandaddy, how have you lived with her all these years?"[122]

• Famed conductor Arturo Toscanini asked his granddaughter, Sonia Horowitz, whose father was the famed pianist Vladimir Horowitz, whether she would prefer to be a conductor like her grandfather or a pianist like her father. She answered, "A conductor—because it's a lot easier."[123]

• When television talk-show host David Letterman was a small child, his grandfather used to take him out to hunt for watermelons. They were always careful to sneak up on the watermelons, because if a watermelon knows you are coming, it will run away.[124]

Halloween

• When ballerina Darci Kistler was five years old, a neighbor gave her a Halloween costume—a pink tutu. Because she knew that she wanted to learn to dance (even at age three, she was cutting photographs of ballerinas out of magazines), she wore the tutu around the house after Halloween as a hint for her mother to sign her up for dance lessons. The hint worked.[125]

120. Source: Anne Schraff, *Ralph Bunche: Winner of the Nobel Peace Prize*, p. 22.
121. Source: Frank DeCaro, *A Boy Named Phyllis*, p. 24.
122. Source: Jerry Clower, *Life Everlaughter*, pp. 53-54.
123. Source: David Ewen, *Listen to the Mocking Words*, pp. 77-78.
124. Source: Bill Adler, *The Letterman Wit: His Life and Humor*, pp. 10-11.
125. Source: Darci Kistler, *Ballerina: My Story*, pp. 19, 99.

Husbands and Wives

• Just after the end of World War II, while country comedian Archie Campbell was still an enlisted man in the United States Navy, he hadn't seen his wife for a long time, so he asked Lieutenant Sam Bailey if a way could be arranged for him to see her. Therefore, Lieutenant Bailey asked Mr. Campbell to take an apparatus to Florida to have it repaired—of course, Mr. Campbell had his wife meet him in Florida. At the repair shop, Mr. Campbell asked how long it would take to have the apparatus repaired, and the technician assured him that it would be repaired by the very next day. This was bad news for Mr. Campbell and his wife, so he explained the situation to the technician, saying, "I haven't seen my wife in over a year. Take longer than that." The technician replied, "In that case, it will take at least a week."[126]

• As a world-class track athlete, Thelma Wright competed away from home, meaning long separations from her husband, Lee. And even when her husband was nearby, practices, competitions, and media interviews sometimes kept her from seeing him. At the 1972 Olympic Games, many fans asked for her autograph and gave her pieces of papers to sign. While she was surrounded by autograph-seeking fans one day, someone gave her a crumpled piece of paper. She looked up to see who had given her the paper—it was her husband, who said, "Hi, I just wanted to say hello."[127]

• Hugh Downs and his wife were in Washington. D.C. While Mr. Downs' wife was in the shower, he received a telephone call saying that their flight to New York had been cancelled because of bad weather. However, after making a telephone call, he discovered that a train would be leaving soon for New York. So he quickly packed all of his and his wife's clothing and had it sent to the train station. Just then, his wife came into the bedroom with a towel wrapped around her. "Dear," she said, "would you please hand me my green dress?"[128]

• A housewife once bought some guest towels for a party. She hung them up in the bathroom, but being afraid that her husband would use the towels before the party started, she hung a sign on them: "If you use these towels, I'll kill you." Then she went around the house, making other preparations. The party seemed to go well, but when it was over, she noticed that none of the guests had used the guest towels—she had forgotten to take down the sign.[129]

---

126. Source: Archie Campbell, *Archie Campbell: An Autobiography*, pp. 81-82.
127. Source: Diana C. Gleasner, *Track and Field*, pp. 22-23.
128. Source: Gerald Fuller, *Stories for All Seasons*, p. 41.
129. Source: Art Linkletter, *Oops!*, pp. 67-68.

• When Constance Samwell was secretly engaged to her future husband, Frank Benson, she sometimes heard two actresses discussing in the dressing room which of them would marry him. Sometimes, one of the actresses would say that Mr. Benson had walked her home and stayed with her until late—but Ms. Samwell knew that Mr. Benson had walked her home that particular night and stayed with her until late. (Later, Constance and Frank were married.)[130]

• Jane Stevenson learned that her police officer husband was a transvestite on their wedding night. He came out of the bathroom wearing a white embroidered peignoir that was prettier than what she was wearing. On his face was an imploring look that said, "Please understand me." She put her arms around him, and she said, "I love you." He said, "I can't help this." She replied, "You don't have to explain. I love you. Tonight you don't have to explain. I accept it."[131]

• In his old age, Moe Howard of Three Stooges fame guested on TV's *Mike Douglas Show*. At one point, Mr. Douglas asked Moe if he had "any unfulfilled ambitions." Moe got a gleam in his eye, grabbed a pie (when you're a Stooge, one is always handy), charged straight into the audience, and hit his wife smack in the face with the pie. His wife, Helen, took it well, saying, "Moe's been rehearsing for that all his life. I'm glad he finally got it out of his system."[132]

• In the 16th century, Irishwoman Elizabeth Fitzgerald was surrounded by enemies who told her that they had captured her husband and would hang him unless she surrendered her castle immediately. Standing on the battlements of her castle, Ms. Fitzgerald shouted, "Mark these words—they may serve your own wives on some occasion. I'll keep my castle; for Elizabeth Fitzgerald may get another husband, but Elizabeth Fitzgerald may never get another castle."[133]

• Henny Youngman's most famous joke was written by accident. Once, he was preparing for a stint on the Kate Smith radio show, when his wife and some of her friends came backstage to visit him. Unfortunately, because of their talking, Mr. Youngman wasn't able to concentrate on his preparation, so he decided to have someone take his wife and her friends to sit in the audience. Finding a stagehand, he told him, "Take my wife—please![134]

• Israel Zangwill married a non-Jew in 1901, upsetting many Jews. Shortly after his marriage, he spoke before a large Jewish audience. Worried about how his wife would be treated, he said to the audience, "Fellow Jews, I trust you will

130. Source: Constance Benson, *Mainly Players*, pp. 52-53.
131. Source: Zsa Zsa Gershick, *Gay Old Girls*, p. 8.
132. Source: Morris "Moe" Feinberg, *Larry: The Stooge in the Middle*, pp. 204, 206.
133. Source: Sean McCann, compiler, *The Wit of the Irish*, p. 40.
134. Source: Henny Youngman, *Take My Life, Please!*, p. 21.

be courteous to Mrs. Zangwill, and that you will not do or say anything that might offend her. While I may deserve censure for marrying a Gentile, Mrs. Zangwill deserves nothing but praise—she married a Jew."[135]

• Elizabeth Barrett Browning's *Sonnets from the Portuguese* were poems intended to be read only by her husband, Robert Browning, but because of their high quality, he insisted that they be published. The sonnets were not translated from Portuguese. Instead, the poems received this particular title because Mr. Browning called his wife, who had a dark complexion, "my little Portuguese."[136]

• When African-American comedian Dick Gregory became a stand-up comedian, he knew that eventually someone in the audience would call him a nigger, so he practiced controlling his reaction by having his wife yell "nigger" at him at home. When it finally happened in a nightclub, Mr. Gregory had his response ready: "You hear what that guy just called me? Roy Rogers' horse. He called me Trigger."[137]

• Mark Twain liked to visit neighbors informally—without wearing a collar or tie. This upset his wife, Livy, so Mr. Twain wrapped up a package which he sent to his neighbors along with a note that read: "A little while ago, I visited you for about half an hour minus my collar and tie. The missing articles are enclosed. Will you kindly gaze at them for 30 minutes and then return them to me?"[138]

• Anne Sexton once wrote a volume of poetry titled *Love Poems*. One poem was intended to be titled "Twenty-One Days Without You" because her career required her to spend that amount of time away from her husband. However, the title had to be changed to "Eighteen Days Without You" after her husband said to her, "I can't stand it any longer; you haven't been with me for days."[139]

• Robert Dole and his wife, Elizabeth, once made the bed while posing for *People* magazine. When the photographs were published, a man wrote Senator Dole, complaining that he was making things tough for men all over the country. Senator Dole wrote back, "You don't know the half of it. The only reason she was helping was because they were taking pictures."[140]

• Journalist Heywood Broun met and married Ruth Hale, who was also a journalist. On their first date, they walked in the park, where a squirrel came up to them and begged for food. Ms. Hale told Mr. Broun that she wished she had

135. Source: Lawrence J. Epstein, *A Treasury of Jewish Anecdotes*, p. 251.
136. Source: André Bernard, *Now All We Need is a Title*, p. 23.
137. Source: Phil Berger, *The Last Laugh*, p. 122.
138. Source: Lewis C. Henry, *Humorous Anecdotes About Famous People*, pp. 37-38.
139. Source: André Bernard, *Now All We Need is a Title*, p. 76.
140. Source: Bob Dole, *Great Political Wit*, pp. 75-76.

some nuts for the squirrel, and Mr. Broun replied, "I can't help you except to give him a nickel so he can go and buy his own."[141]

• Donald Grey Barnhouse, a pastor, once stayed at the house of an Australian man who had married an American woman. Before the two were married, the woman had never allowed her future husband to kiss her, so their first kiss took place before the altar of the church. "But," said her husband, "after I got the first one, the rest came easy."[142]

• Terence Grey, the owner of a British theater, once heard that his wife was having an affair. He rushed home, grabbed an axe, used it to beat his way through the bedroom door, and stood with the axe raised in front of the bed, on which lay his cowering wife and her cowering lover. Then he lowered the axe and stuck out his tongue at them.[143]

• Rusty Kothavala was a proctor and instructor at Harvard. After getting married and fathering a daughter, he discovered he was gay and began frequenting gay bars. When he eventually told his wife, she was very understanding: "Is that all? Here I thought you were one of these international criminals or something."[144]

• The wife of Albert Einstein, the great physicist and mathematician, once toured the Mt. Wilson Observatory in California, where her tour guide explained that all this expensive, modern equipment was being used to "find out the shape of the universe." Mrs. Einstein replied, "Oh, my husband does that on the back of an old envelope."[145]

• Harry Belafonte talked about his family while he was on *The Mike Douglas Show*, mentioning that his oldest child was 24 years old. When Mike Douglas asked how long he had been married, he answered, "Seventeen years." Mr. Douglas began to count on his fingers, and Mr. Belafonte added, "Hey, I've been married before."[146]

• Anna Pavlova, in addition to being a dancer, was also a wife. People going backstage at the New York Metropolitan Opera House were once treated to the sight of Ms. Pavlova throwing ballet slippers at the back of her retreating husband, Victor Dandré, while she shouted at him in Russian.[147]

141. Source: Robert E. Drennan, editor, *The Algonquin Wits*, p. 64.
142. Source: Donald Grey Barnhouse, *Let Me Illustrate*, p. 36.
143. Source: Robert Morley, *Around the World in Eighty-One Years*, p. 33.
144. Source: Andrew Tobias, *The Best Little Boy in the World Grows Up*, pp. 13-14.
145. Source: Kenneth Williams, *Acid Drops*, p. 74.
146. Source: Kermit Schafer, *All Time Great Bloopers*, p. 88.
147. Source: A.H. Franks, editor, *Pavlova: A Collection of Memoirs*, p. 58.

• During World War I, dancer Ted Shawn joined the United States Army. His wife, Ruth St. Denis, performed for the troops, then the next day watched a parade in which her husband took part. When Ms. St. Denis was asked what she thought of the parade, she replied, "Oh, I thought *he* was grand."[148]

• Mark Twain enjoyed reading and writing in bed. One day, a reporter was coming over to interview him, so his wife, Livy, said, "Don't you think it would be a bit embarrassing for the reporter—your being in bed?" Mr. Twain replied, "Why, Livy, if you think so, we might have the other bed made up for him."[149]

• Stand-up comedian Rita Rudner used to do a lot of jokes about being single, and when she got married, she worried about losing 20 minutes of comic material. Still, she was glad she got married. In fact, she says, "For him, I would have given up 40 minutes."[150]

• Jack Gilford's wife, Madeline, had been married before. She remained married for eight years, then got a divorce. On his eighth anniversary, Mr. Gilford told a friend, "I better run home and see if my option has been picked up."[151]

Illness

• The late Mister Rogers really did answer his fan mail—as is shown by the book, *Dear Mister Rogers, Does It Ever Rain in Your Neighborhood?* One letter was from a mother whose daughter, Michelle—only 5 1/2 years old—needed radiation treatment for an inoperable brain tumor. Michelle refused to undergo the treatment because she had to be alone, even though the treatment would last just one minute. After a few days of refusing the treatment, Michelle asked, "What's a minute?" Her mother answered by singing part of Mister Rogers' theme song, "It's a Beautiful Day in the Neighborhood," and said, "Oops! The minute is up. I can't even finish Mister Rogers' song." Michelle then exclaimed, "Is that a minute? I can do that!"—and did.[152]

• While researching a book on children surviving cancer, Erma Bombeck was impressed by the way a three-year-old boy faced life. The boy told her, "You know what? I'm going to the circus!"—but a camp counselor reminded the boy that he wasn't going to the circus, but he was going swimming instead. The boy then turned to Ms. Bombeck and said, "You know what? I'm going swimming!"

---

148. Source: Ted Shawn, *One Thousand and One Night Stands*, p. 81.

149. Source: Cyril Clemens, editor, *Mark Twain Anecdotes*, p. 20.

150. Source: Hank Gallo, *Comedy Explosion: A New Generation*, p. 75.

151. Source: Kate Mostel and Madeline Gilford, *170 Years of Show Business*, p. 127.

152. Source: Fred Rogers, *Dear Mister Rogers, Does It Ever Rain in Your Neighborhood? Letters to Mister Rogers*, pp. 67-68.

Ms. Bombeck wrote later, "It didn't matter, he would have gone to the opening of a bottle of aspirin. And it made me think—little things, little moments. Go for them."[153]

• Albert III, Al Gore's six-year-old son, was hit by a car in 1989 and thrown for several feet, breaking some of his bones and crushing some of his internal organs. He was rushed to a hospital, and when he regained consciousness, he told his parents, "I can't get well without you." They stayed with him throughout his three-week hospital stay, and when they took him home in a full-body cast, they put a bed for him in the dining room and took turns sleeping on a mattress placed on the floor by his bed until he recovered.[154]

• Many people fear AIDS. Carmine Buete was a 10-year-old boy suffering from AIDS who lived with his grandmother near New Year City. After some of the friends of his grandmother discovered that he had AIDS, they refused to talk to her anymore. Because of that experience, Carmine and his grandmother soon learned not to tell many people that he had AIDS. Before he died, one of Carmine's favorite toys was an E.T. doll that made him feel better when he was ill.[155]

• Teddy Kennedy, Jr., the senator's son, lost a leg to cancer in 1973. He used humor to deal with his prothesis (artificial limb). While he was riding on the back of a friend's bicycle, they crashed, and young Ted's foot became twisted around backwards. No problem. He simply twisted his foot around so it was facing the right way, then he walked away. The people watching him—who didn't know he was wearing a prosthesis—were shocked.[156]

In-Laws

• Mark Twain married a woman from a wealthy family. Arriving in Buffalo, New York, Mr. and Mrs. Twain were driven to a mansion, where his new wife told Mr. Twain that the mansion was a gift to them from her father. Mr. Twain shook hands with his father-in-law, then said, "If you ever come to Buffalo, bring your grip [suitcase] and stay all night—it won't cost you a cent."[157]

• A 1993 TV commercial for a Norwegian airline showed a man stripping until he was wearing nothing but his socks, then bursting through a doorway to surprise his wife. Unfortunately, her parents are with her—and they know don't

153. Source: Susan Edwards, *Erma Bombeck*, p. 182.
154. Source: JoAnn Bren Guernsey, *Tipper Gore: Voice for the Voiceless*, pp. 39-40.
155. Source: Arlene Schulman, *Carmine's Story*, pp. 8, 15.
156. Source: Erma Bombeck, *I Want to Grow Hair, I Want to Grow Up, I Want to Go to Boise*, p. 92.
157. Source: Cyril Clemens, editor, *Mark Twain Anecdotes*, p. 9.

where to look. The title card for the commercial says, "Warning: we're flying in your in-laws at half-price."[158]

• Irish ballad writer Jimmy Hiney is a small man. When he was first introduced to his mother-in-law, she told her daughter, "Well, by God, if you get nothing else from him, you'll always get a laugh."[159]

Language

• As the writer of most episodes of *The Twilight Zone*, host Rod Serling displayed a love of language, a love that he exhibited even as a child. When he was six years old, his family took a two-and-a-half-hour car trip from Binghamton, New York, to Syracuse, New York. Before the trip, his parents agreed that they would not speak until young Rod had stopped talking. However, they never got a chance to speak during the trip because Rod never stopped talking![160]

• After being divorced from his father, Zack's mother, Aimee, discovered that she was in love with another woman, Margie, and they moved in together. Zack occasionally hears other people use words such as "fag" and "dyke," but his mother tells him, "The problem is not with us. It's with them. We're in a family where everybody loves each other, and that's what matters."[161]

Money

• Wilson Mizner once married a rich society lady, which seemed to be a marriage made in Heaven, given Mr. Mizner's great delight in spending money. However, his wife kept a tight grip on her money, giving her husband very little of it. Mr. Mizner once got on his knees and pleaded for an hour with his wife to prove her love for him by signing a blank check, but she would not. While dining at the Waldorf-Astoria, Mr. Mizner was again pleading for money. This so annoyed his wife that she began beating him with the nearest thing she had in her possession—an envelope filled with money. The envelope came open, the money spilled everywhere, and Mr. Mizner and the other diners in the restaurant began scrambling for it. His wife saw him on his knees, picking up money, and screamed that he could have the money since he was willing to crawl for it. Mr. Mizner said later, "I'd picked up $8,000 before I realized I'd been insulted."[162]

---

158. Source: Bernice Kanner, *The 100 Best TV Commercials*, p. 180.

159. Source: Sean McCann, compiler, *The Wit of the Irish*, p. 71.

160. Source: Bob Madison, *American Horror Writers*, p. 50.

161. Source: Keith Elliot Greenberg, *Zack's Story*, p. 7.

• When Pulitzer Prize-winning reporter Meyer Berger was a boy, his family was poor in money. One day early in the 20th century, he announced to his mother that he had been given the honor of making an acceptance speech because a local organization was donating a new flag to his school. Of course, this was good news, but his mother looked at his shoes and was embarrassed. She told the family that they had only 25 cents, and either she could use the money to buy Meyer a used pair of shoes so he could be decently dressed when he made the acceptance speech, or she could put it in the gas meter and the family could eat a hot supper. The family voted for the shoes, and they ate a cold supper that night. After young Meyer had made his acceptance speech at school, he repeated it at home so his family could hear him.[163]

• Author Donald Ogden Stewart's son once broke a window. Since Mr. Stewart had to go to work at a movie studio on a Sunday, he tried to use the occasion to make his son feel guilty for breaking the window by saying that Daddy had to go to work to pay for the broken window instead of playing tennis, as he had hoped. Mr. Stewart asked his son, "Aren't you sorry that poor, dear Daddy has to work on his day off, just because of you?" His son replied, "If you have any money left over, buy me an air rifle."[164]

• In 1934, Will Rogers starred in *Ah, Wilderness*, a play by Eugene O'Neill. However, after he received a letter from a minister telling him that this particular play was unsuitable for being seen by families, Mr. Rogers declined to star in the movie version of the play, thereby losing a salary of over $200,000—a sum that is approximately $2 million in year 2000 money.[165]

• When Eugene Field was a student at Knox College, he sometimes telegraphed his guardian, Melvin L. Gray, for money. If the requested money was slow in arriving, Mr. Field would telegraph Mr. Gray again, saying that unless he received some money quickly, he would be forced to go into show business and bill himself as "Melvin L. Gray, Banjo and Specialty Artist."[166]

Mothers

• George Burns loved his mother and regarded her as a wonderful problem-solver. For example, when one of his sisters, Mamie, and her husband, Dr. Max

---

162. Source: John Burke, *Rogue's Progress: The Fabulous Adventures of Wilson Mizner*, pp. 94-95, 98-99.

163. Source: Mildred and Milton Lewis, *Famous Modern Newspaper Writers*, pp. 32-33.

164. Source: J. Bryan III, *Merry Gentlemen (and One Lady)*, p. 159.

165. Source: Mary Malone, *Will Rogers: Cowboy Philosopher*, p. 108.

166. Source: H. Allen Smith, *The Compleat Practical Joker*, p. 256.

Salis, were having problems and considering getting a divorce, his mother called in her daughter and listened to her side of the story. Then she told her daughter, "Mamie, you're wrong and the doctor is right. I want you to apologize to Max. Tell him you're sorry and that it won't happen again." After Mamie had left, his mother called in Max and told him, "Doctor, Mamie was right. Don't ever do that again."[167]

• Faye Zealand, as part of the AIDS Resource Foundation for Children, has much experience not just with children who have HIV or AIDS, but with children whose parents have died from AIDS. She knows one little girl who wanted a photograph of her mother, who had died from AIDS. Her foster mother got her a photo, but other people were in it, and the little girl asked for a photo showing only her mother. After she received this photo, the little girl would put it on top of her pillow at night, placing it so that it touched her head—only then would she go to sleep.[168]

• When David Letterman is in Indiana, he visits his mother. Once, he called his mother to let her know he was coming over, and when he arrived at her house, she asked him, "David, would you like some strawberry pie?" He saw a freshly baked strawberry pie on a table, so he asked her, "When did you make this?" She replied, "I started right after I got off the phone with you." Mr. Letterman was pleased: "It was just the cutest. I was so touched. Isn't that motherhood? She gets off the phone, drops what she's doing, and *bakes a pie.*"[169]

• When Olympic gold medal gymnast Bart Conner and his brothers were growing up, they had a lot of gymnastics equipment, including a set of parallel bars in the basement and a set of rings in the yard. Their mother was afraid they would hurt themselves, so occasionally she would drive around looking for discarded mattresses the day before the trash was picked up. When she found one, she would ask if she could have it, and she would take it home and place it under the gymnastics equipment.[170]

• As a single mother, Mary Jane Kurtz found it difficult to get her children ready on time to go to church. One Sunday morning, she told her children to get ready in no uncertain terms and they started laughing at her. They told her, "Mom, every time you slam down your foot, smoke comes out. It must be the wrath of God!" The smoke was actually the powder she had put in her shoes, but thereafter her children got ready on time to go to church.[171]

167. Source: Tim Boxer, *The Jewish Celebrity Hall of Fame*, pp. 47-48.
168. Source: Michael Thomas Ford, *The Voices of AIDS*, pp. 84-85.
169. Source: Bill Adler, *The Letterman Wit: His Life and Humor*, p. 98.
170. Source: Bart Conner, *Winning the Gold*, p. 11.

• Twyla Tharp's mother had great faith in her daughter. Whenever Twyla brought home a report card that carried any grade lower than an A-, her mother immediately assumed that her daughter's teacher was incompetent and made arrangements for Twyla to attend a different class—and sometimes a different school. Later, Twyla became the world-famous choreographer of *Push Comes to Shove*.[172]

• English entertainer Joyce Grenfell was an actress who played a series of unglamorous roles in the movies, disappointing her mother, who wanted Joyce to be glamorous. Once, her mother told a friend that her daughter was in a movie that they were going to see, but when she saw Joyce in yet another unglamorous role, she told her friend that she had been mistaken and her daughter wasn't in the movie.[173]

• Comedian W.C. Fields was good to his mother. After leaving home, he studied juggling and comedy. Once he began to make good, he sent his mother a note and a $10 bill in December of 1898, and thereafter he sent her at least $10 a week. However, in keeping with his comic persona, he didn't let people know what he was doing, and he always denied that he would ever help his family.[174]

• Parents sometimes are shocked to learn that one of their children is gay, but often they quickly adjust—usually after spending some time wondering whether they caused their child's homosexuality. One mother went through that process, but eventually joked to her gay son, "I finally figured out why you are gay—I chewed Juicy Fruit gum while I was pregnant with you."[175]

• As part of the Kinaaldá ceremony that marks a Navajo girl's coming of age, the girl's mother "molds" her with her hands into the shape of a beautiful and strong woman. When Celinda McKelvey's mother molded her, she squeezed her stomach "so you don't grow up to be fat." Smiling, Celinda asked her mother to do it again—"just to make sure I stay skinny."[176]

• When author Frank DeCaro's mother decided to learn to drive, she asked her brother to teach her. He immediately drove his car to the top of the steepest hill in town, got himself and his dog out of the car, then told her, "Go ahead. Drive." Decades later, she still complained, "Can you believe he took his dog with him?"[177]

171. Source: Edward K. Rowell, editor, *Humor for Preaching and Teaching*, p. 80.
172. Source: Carin T. Ford, *Legends of American Dance and Choreography*, p. 83.
173. Source: Joyce Grenfell, *Joyce Grenfell Requests the Pleasure*, p. 245.
174. Source: Robert Lewis Taylor, *W.C. Fields: His Follies and Fortunes*, p. 61.
175. Source: Chastity Bono, *Family Outing*, pp. 92-93.
176. Source: Monty Roessel, *Kinaaldá: A Navajo Girl Grows Up*, p. 22.

• Eve Arden appeared in a play titled *The Road to Rome*, about the Carthaginian general Hannibal. Once, when Hannibal's soldiers roughly dragged Ms. Arden's character away on stage, the voice of Liza, Ms. Arden's two-year-old daughter, could be heard in the audience, asking, "What are those men doing to my mommy?"[178]

• When comedian Bob Smith came out to his mother, she said, "You're gay…well, it could be worse. Look at the Gardiners across the street with those retarded grandchildren." Mr. Smith laughed and said, "Thanks, Mom. I love that comparison." Shortly afterward, she wrote him a loving letter of acceptance.[179]

• As a young boy, Bart Conner was already into gymnastics. Often, he used to come home from school, and talk to his mother while he was standing on his head. Once, while he was standing on his head, she stood on *her* head and they talked to each other.[180]

• Figure skater Peggy Fleming keeps scrapbooks filled with photographs of her family and children in a cabinet near her garage door. Why? If her house is ever threatened by fire, she wants her photographs handy so she can save them.[181]

Music

• Before her marriage, soprano Frances Alda had many beaus. Once, four of her beaus showed up on the same day to hear her perform at the Metropolitan Opera. Each beau told her where he would be sitting at the Met. During the course of the opera, Ms. Alda sang in turn to each part of the Met where she knew one of her beaus would be sitting. By the time the opera was over, she had convinced each beau that she had been singing especially to him.[182]

• Ballerina Suzanne Farrell and her choreographer husband, Paul Mejia, bought an island in a lake in the Adirondack Mountains and turned it into a dance camp. Often, local tourist boats would cruise past the island, which the tour guides called "Ballerina Island." A nearby local couple ate their dinners during the early ballet class so they could enjoy the romantic music.[183]

• John von Neumann was a child prodigy, but not in music. His parents made him take music lessons, but they were surprised at his lack of improvement. Then

---

177. Source: Frank DeCaro, *A Boy Named Phyllis*, pp. 7-8.
178. Source: Eve Arden, *Three Phases of Eve*, p. 70.
179. Source: Bob Smith, *Openly Bob*, p. 180.
180. Source: Bart Conner, *Winning the Gold*, pp. 7-8.
181. Source: Christine Brennan, *Inside Edge*, p. 168.
182. Source: Frances Alda, *Men, Women, and Tenors*, p. 101.
183. Source: Suzanne Farrell, *Holding On to the Air*, pp. 258-259.

they discovered that as their son practiced music scales on his cello, he was reading a science or history book that he had placed on his music stand.[184]

Old Age

• Paul Douglas used to be a United States senator. When he was old, he suffered a stroke and was confined to a wheelchair. One day, while reaching for something, he fell out of his wheelchair. The only other person at home was his wife, who wasn't strong enough to pick him up and put him back in the wheelchair. She told her husband, "Paul, we haven't had a picnic in such a long time," then she went into the kitchen and made some sandwiches. She brought out the sandwiches, put a few potted plants around to make the scene look more like the country, then opened a bottle of wine. The two had their picnic, then they read love poetry to each other until someone arrived to help pick up Mr. Douglas.[185]

• An aged parent had a problem, so he asked R' Shmuel Salant for advice. The problem was this: His sons had moved to America, and now they did not keep the Sabbath or observe the other commandments that God had given His chosen people. However, his sons did send him money, and he worried whether it was proper to accept the money. R' Shmuel Salant said, "Your sons wish to keep only one commandment, that of honoring their parents, and you wish to deprive them of that as well?"[186]

• All his life, Rabbi Moshe Feinstein got up each day at 4 a.m. in order to study. When he was 85, his wife pleaded with him to get up a little later, so that he could rest more, but he replied that he needed to get up that early to study because he didn't want to remain an ignoramus.[187]

Olympics

• United States figure skater Tara Lipinski has wanted to win a medal at the Olympics ever since she was a child. When she was still a toddler, the Olympics were on TV, but she didn't pay much attention until some medals were awarded—then she was fascinated. She watched the athletes stand on podiums, wearing ribbons around their necks and holding flowers. Tara's parents used to keep her toys in Tupperware containers, so to create a podium, she turned over

---

184. Source: Mary Northrup, *American Computer Pioneers*, p. 20.
185. Source: Maury Maverick, Jr., *Texas Iconoclast*, pp. 233-234.
186. Source: Shmuel Himelstein, *A Touch of Wisdom, A Touch of Wit*, p. 187.
187. Source: Shmuel Himelstein, *Words of Wisdom, Words of Wit*, p. 36.

one of the Tupperware containers and stood on it, then she asked her mother for a ribbon and some flowers so she could be like the athletes on TV.[188]

• Strange things sometimes happen to child athletes. When she was nine years old, Russian figure skater Ekaterina Gordeeva began to skate in a competition, but she discovered that she could not move her head because she had accidentally zipped her hair in her costume. She had to stop skating so she could unzip her ponytail. As an adult, she won two Olympic gold medals in pairs skating with her husband, Sergei Grinkov.[189]

• As a young gymnast, Dominic Moceanu showed a lot of confidence. While signing autographs before the 1996 Olympic Games in Atlanta were held, she added to her signature, "'96 gold, for sure." Her cockiness was justified—the United States women's gymnastics team, of which Ms. Moceanu was a member, won the gold medal.[190]

• After Dorothy Hamill won the gold medal in women's figure skating at the 1976 Olympic Games, she slept with it under her pillow. The next day, someone asked where she was keeping it. She pulled it from out of her blouse and said, "Right here."[191]

Parents

• Tara Lipinski is a champion figure skater, but her parents had to sacrifice for her to become a champion. Her father lived in Texas, where his job is, but Tara and her mother lived in Detroit, where she could train with a top coach and skate at a top rink. In addition, her parents refinanced their house and took out a loan to pay for Tara's skating, coaching, and travel expenses. Now that Tara is an Olympic gold medalist and a professional figure skater, she earns enough money by performing to more than pay for her expenses. (The parents of many other champion sports stars also make these kinds of sacrifices.)[192]

• Zack lives in New Jersey and has same-sex parents—Aimee and Margie. One day, he was talking with his friend Alex and they stopped talking when Zack's mother and her lover—Zack calls them his two mothers—walked up to them. Curious, Zack's mother, Aimee, asked what was going on. Alex replied, "I wanted to know if it's all right if I told someone that you're a lesbian." Aimee

188. Source: Tara Lipinski and Emily Costello, *Tara Lipinski: Triumph on Ice*, pp. 3-4.
189. Source: Ekaterina Gordeeva, *My Sergei*, pp. 24-25.
190. Source: Kerri Strug, *Landing on My Feet*, p. 132.
191. Source: S.H. Burchard, *Dorothy Hamill*, p. 53.
192. Source: Tara Lipinski, *Tara Lipinski: Triumph on Ice*, pp. 23-24.

looked at Margie for a moment, then the two women laughed, and Aimee said, "Sure, it's all right. We like being lesbians."[193]

• Parents worry about their teenage children going out on dates, and they want to meet the people their children are dating. A mother was shocked when her daughter said she was going on a date with a boy the mother had not met, so the girl's mother decided to call the boy's mother to find out something about him. The boy's mother stated, "He's my son, and I love him." Hearing that, the girl's mother sighed and said, "Well, that's fine. I'm sure everything will be all right."[194]

• Some teachers can get upset with parents. Following one conference with a mother, a Quaker teacher exclaimed, "The only people who ought not to have children are parents!" A former head of Bootham School, a school for Quakers, once said, "There are moments when I feel that in the next world I would like to be Head Master of an orphanage."[195]

• When Mexican artist Diego Rivera was a small child, he liked to draw on walls and furniture. Of course, his parents didn't want him to do this, but they did want him to use his creativity, so his father set aside an entire room for young Diego. He covered the entire room with canvas, so Diego was able to draw wherever he liked in that room.[196]

• When children compete at important sports events, their parents react in different ways. When Dorothy Hamill won the gold medal in women's figure skating at the 1976 Olympic Games, her father watched the competition in person, but her mother was too nervous to watch and stayed in her hotel room.[197]

• Etiquette expert Grace Fox knows a family that schedules regular musical or literary nights. On one occasion, the parents tried to turn on their children—metalheads all—to the music of the Beatles and Janis Joplin. (Their children remained metalheads, but everyone had fun.)[198]

• When he was growing up, professional baseball player Harmon Killebrew used to play ball with his brother and father in the front yard. His mother once complained that they were ruining the lawn, but his father replied, "We're raising kids—not raising grass."[199]

193. Source: Keith Elliot Greenberg, *Zack's Story*, pp. 4-5, 10.
194. Source: Norton Mockridge, *A Funny Thing Happened…*, p. 20.
195. Source: William H. Sessions, collector, *More Quaker Laughter*, p. 99.
196. Source: Doreen Gonzales, *Diego Rivera: His Art, His Life*, p. 21.
197. Source: S.H. Burchard, *Dorothy Hamill*, p. 48.
198. Source: Grace Fox, *Everyday Etiquette*, p. 25.
199. Source: Joe Garagiola, *It's Anybody's Ballgame*, p. 272.

• Trevor Mark Sage-EL is a bi-racial child growing up in New Jersey. His father is black, and his mother is white. When people ask Trevor what he is, he replies, "Human." And when he thinks it is necessary, he asks, "What are you? Alien?"[200]

Physicians

• Leila Denmark, born 1898, was still practicing pediatric medicine at age 100. Her advice often drew on her long experience in life. Once, a mother called Dr. Denmark after her two children had gotten pinworm. Dr. Denmark told her that it wasn't anything to worry about and to bring the children to her clinic on Monday. Then Dr. Denmark asked why the mother was crying. After learning that she was crying because her husband was blaming her for the children's contracting pinworm, Dr. Denmark made a prescription: "You go gather the family up, and everybody go on a picnic today."[201]

• A man was doing minor repairs around the house, and he decided to revarnish the toilet seat. Unfortunately, he forgot to tell his wife, and a short time later, he heard her calling from the bathroom, "I'm stuck!" Unable to free his wife, the man unbolted the toilet seat and carried both her and it to the bedroom, where he placed her face down on the bed, then called their physician. The physician arrived, surveyed the situation, then said, "I agree that it's very pretty, but why did you decide to frame it?"[202]

Practical Jokes

• When Al Gore was appearing on the TV program *Larry King Live*, his wife, Tipper, phoned in and, disguising her voice, said, "I just had to tell you—you're the most handsome man I've ever seen." Still disguising her voice, she asked him for a date. Mr. Gore didn't recognize her voice, so he was embarrassed as he tried to stammer out an answer. Finally, Mr. King pointed out that Mr. Gore was a married man and so of course he wouldn't be willing to make a date. Using her own voice, Mrs. Gore then asked, "Not even with his wife?"[203]

• Comedian Robin Williams' mother had a sense of humor. She once attended an invitational dance at the Lake Forest—Lake Bluff (Illinois) Bath and Tennis Club. She dressed extremely well, but she also blacked out her front teeth,

200. Source: Bethany Kandel, *Trevor's Story*, p. 7.
201. Source: Jeanne Marie Laskas, *We Remember*, p. 59.
202. Source: Harvey Mindess, *The Chosen People?*, pp. 76-77.
203. Source: JoAnn Bren Guernsey, *Tipper Gore: Voice for the Voiceless*, pp. 58-59.

making herself appear toothless. All around her, people were saying, "You'd think someone who could afford clothes like that could afford to get her teeth fixed."[204]

• Beatrice Kaufman once asked Alexander Woollcott to write a reference letter so her daughter could attend a certain school. As a joke, Mr. Woollcott sent to Mrs. Kaufman what she took to be a carbon copy of his reference letter, which began, "I implore you to accept this unfortunate child and remove her from her shocking environment."[205]

Prejudice

• As a bi-racial child, Trevor Mark Sage-EL is aware of racism. His father is black, and his mother is white. When his parents needed a loan to buy a house, they went together to a bank, where their loan application was turned down. So the next time his mother went alone to the bank, and this time their loan application was accepted. Trevor also is aware that his family is treated differently when he is alone with his father than when he is alone with his mother. Once, a woman thought that his father, who was eating a hamburger, was going to steal her purse. That kind of thing doesn't happen when Trevor is alone with his mother.[206]

• Families change. Two parents discovered that their young son was gay, and they took the news so badly that their son ran away for a year. They were overwhelmed with remorse and did their best to track their son down. Eventually, they discovered that he was in Portland, so they went to the police there for help, but the woman police officer the father first contacted immediately told him that homosexuality is wrong. The father told her, "I don't give a damn how you feel about it. This is my son and I need to find him—he's 15 years old."[207]

Problem-Solving

• A couple of American teachers who were best friends went on a trip to Mexico. Walking along a street, they were arrested and taken to the police station, where they discovered that they had been walking in a red-light district in which the only women allowed were licensed prostitutes. The fine for a woman without a prostitute's license walking there was 20,000 pesos. Like most teachers, the women didn't have much money, and what money they did have, they wanted to spend on their vacation, not on a fine. Fortunately, they found a way out of their

---

204. Source: Jay David, *The Life and Humor of Robin Williams*, p. 3.
205. Source: Robert E. Drennan, editor, *The Algonquin Wits*, p. 148.
206. Source: Bethany Kandel, *Trevor's Story*, p. 22.
207. Source: Chastity Bono, *Family Outing*, pp. 212-213.

dilemma: In order not to spend good money on a fine, and with no thought of taking up a new profession, each teacher avoided the fine by purchasing a prostitute's license for 20 pesos.[208]

• When he was a child, John W. Mauchly liked to read in bed at night, but his mother wanted him to get his sleep, so she sometimes checked to make sure that his light was out. Therefore, he invented a special lamp to solve this problem. When his mother came up the stairs to check on him, the lamp automatically went out. When she went down the stairs after checking up on him, the lamp automatically came on again. As an adult, Mr. Mauchly became one of the co-designers of the ENIAC and UNIVAC computers.[209]

• Buddy and Vilma Ebsen were a famous brother-and-sister dance team during the 1930s. They danced to arrangements by Glenn Miller, who put a lot of brass into the arrangements. Sometimes, the brass players in small towns would object to playing the arrangements, so Buddy would ask his sister, "Would you go give them your bass-section smile?"[210]

• Joe E. Brown's household was filled with milk drinkers—they drank 17 quarts a day. Because there were so many milk drinkers in the family, there often wasn't any left for Mr. Brown to have a glass late at night after returning home from work. His wife solved the problem by putting the sign "POISON—DON'T DRINK" on one bottle each day.[211]

Public Speaking

• William Jennings Bryan ran for President of the United States against William F. McKinley. While on the campaign trail, Mr. Bryan made a speech in which he told his audience that "come November, my wife will be sleeping in the White House." A man in the crowd immediately yelled, "And if she is, she'll be sleeping with McKinley."[212]

• The unmarried daughter of English statesman William Wilberforce campaigned for him. As she rose to speak, the audience chanted, "Miss Wilberforce forever! Miss Wilberforce forever!" She replied, "I thank you, gentlemen, but I do not wish to remain *Miss* Wilberforce forever."[213]

---

208. Source: Logan Munger Brady, *Amusing Anecdotes*, p. 284.
209. Source: Mary Northrup, *American Computer Pioneers*, p. 39.
210. Source: Rusty E. Frank, *Tap!*, pp. 142-143.
211. Source: Joe E. Brown, *Laughter is a Wonderful Thing*, p. 200.
212. Source: Art Linkletter, *Oops!*, pp. x-xi.
213. Source: Lewis C. Henry, *Humorous Anecdotes About Famous People*, p. 132.

Sex

• A 1991 public service TV commercial in Spain showed a high school principal snooping in the locker rooms as students take gym class. The principal walks into the gym, holds a condom up high, and tells the students in a threatening voice, "I found this in your dressing room. Whose is it?" A boy says, "It's mine." Instantly, another boy says, "It's mine." Then a girl says, "It's mine." Suddenly, dozens of students, all of whom resent the principal's snooping, are telling the principal, "It's mine." At this point comes the public service message: "The condom is the most efficient method for preventing unwanted births and sexually transmitted diseases. Put it on. Put it on him."[214]

• As you would expect, Groucho Marx was very good at puncturing the pride of rich people. During World War II, so many men were away fighting that Groucho was forced to do his own gardening. A rich woman saw him, assumed that he was a real gardener, and tried to entice him away from the family that she supposed had hired him. She stopped her car and asked, "Oh, gardener—how much do you get a month?" Groucho replied, "Oh, I don't get paid in dollars—the lady of the house lets me sleep with her." (Of course, Groucho was married to the lady of his house.)[215]

• A wealthy man once walked in his garden, where he saw his gardener and the gardener's beautiful wife. Because the wealthy man wanted to sleep with the gardener's beautiful wife, he sent the gardener on an errand, then told the gardener's wife to shut all the gates of the garden. However, the gardener's wife knew what he was up to, so when she returned, she told him, "I have shut all the gates but one." The wealthy man asked, "Which gate is that?" She replied, "The gate that is between us and God." After hearing her answer, the wealthy man begged her to forgive him.[216]

• A couple of professors at the University of Washington were immensely cool. On their table was prominently displayed a copy of Masters and Johnson's *Human Sexual Response*, which reported the results of their research on sex. Inside was an inscription written by Masters and Johnson themselves: "Thanks for your cooperation."[217]

---

214. Source: Bernice Kanner, *The 100 Best TV Commercials*, p. 199.
215. Source: Arthur Marx, *Life With Groucho*, p. 256.
216. Source: James Fadiman and Robert Frager, *Essential Sufism*, p. 172.
217. Source: Richard Watson, *The Philosopher's Diet*, p. 104.

Siblings

• Buddy Ebsen is perhaps best known for portraying the character of Jed Clampett in the TV series *The Beverly Hillbillies*; however, he and Vilma Ebsen were a popular brother-and-sister dance team in the 1930s. As they toured, their billing changed frequently. Sometimes they were billed as the Ebsens, but at other times they were billed as Vilma and Buddy Ebsen. However, Vilma was upset once when they were billed in two towns in a row as "Buddy Ebsen and Sister Vilma." She even threatened, "If that is not replaced with Vilma and Buddy Ebsen, or The Ebsens, you will be very interested to know that I'm doing the whole act in a nun's habit. If I'm going to be Sister Vilma, then I'll be 'Sister' Vilma!"[218]

• Fortunately, homosexuality is becoming more accepted. Lesbian comedian Kate Clinton was trying to get into a concert featuring Ellen DeGeneres when she had to ask a police officer for help. The police officer asked her a few questions—then he tried to fix her up with his sister![219]

• Quaker William H. Sessions once heard a woman in the Salvation Army say that when she realized that wearing jewelry would cause her to go to hell, she immediately gathered up all her jewelry—and gave it to her sister![220]

• Early in figure skater Rudy Galindo's career, he was financially supported by his sister, Laura. For a while, he affectionately called her the "Bank of Laura."[221]

Sons

• A Jew met a cantor and asked, "What shall I do? My son has decided to convert to Christianity." The cantor replied, "Funny you should ask—my son has also decided to convert." Together they sought their rabbi and asked, "What shall we do? Our sons have decided to convert to Christianity." The rabbi replied, "Funny you should ask—my son has also decided to convert." Together they decided to pray to God: "What shall we do? Our sons have decided to convert to Christianity." Out of Heaven, a mighty voice replied, "Funny you should ask...."[222]

• Poet Nikki Giovanni read frequently to Thomas, her young son, but occasionally she was tired and told him, "Go read it yourself," although he was too

218. Source: Rusty E. Frank, *Tap!*, p. 139.
219. Source: Kate Clinton, *Don't Get Me Started*, pp. 58-59.
220. Source: William H. Sessions, collector, *Laughter in Quaker Grey*, p. 21.
221. Source: Christine Brennan, *Inside Edge*, p. 68.
222. Source: Harvey Mindess, *The Chosen People?*, pp. 38-39.

young to read. One day, she said that to him, and he replied, "OK, I will." Ms. Giovanni said, "But you don't know how to read." However, Thomas proved that he could read by picking up a *New York Times* and reading the headlines out loud to her. Immediately, Ms. Giovanni read a story to him. She explained later, "I didn't want to punish him for having learned to read, by not reading to him."[223]

• Francis Hodgson Burnett, author of *A Little Princess* and *The Secret Garden*, based the title character of her novel *Little Lord Fauntleroy* on her own son, Vivien. In 1937, Vivien Burnett died a hero. Two men and two women were in a craft that overturned in a sound. Vivien maneuvered his yawl to the overturned craft and rescued the two men and two women, then he collapsed and died.[224]

• Yitta Halberstam Mandelbaum used to tell bedtime stories to her son, Eli. For an entire year, each of the bedtime stories she told was about her rabbi, Shlomo Carlebach! Eventually, she collected the stories into a book that her son urged her to title *The Rabbi of Love*. (She used the title *Holy Brother*.)[225]

• Comedian Robin Williams often watched Saturday morning cartoons with Zach, his young son. While watching, Mr. Williams sometimes did funny voices and made funny remarks. Usually, Zach enjoyed this, but sometimes he told his father, "Daddy, don't use that voice. Just be Daddy."[226]

• One day, Beatrice Lillie's son, Bobbie, came in the house after playing in the garden. Ms. Lillie saw the dirt on her son's face and arms and asked what he had been doing. He said, "I've been in the garden playing with the faeries." She replied, "Faeries? Elves, dear."[227]

• Art Linkletter's son, Jack, attended Beverly Hills High School, where he once ran for class president. Because 85 percent of the school's students were Jewish, Jack used the name "Linkletterberg" for campaigning purposes and almost won the election.[228]

Thanksgiving

• According to Totie Fields, her sister, Rosie, was the best cook in the family. Just before one Thanksgiving, Rosie prepared a feast of Jewish dishes—mush-

223. Source: Judith Pinkerton Josephson, *Nikki Giovanni: Poet of the People*, p. 49.
224. Source: Angelica Shirley Carpenter and Jean Shirley, *Frances Hodgson Burnett: Beyond the Secret Garden*, p. 119.
225. Source: Yitta Halberstam Mandelbaum, *Holy Brother*, p. xiv.
226. Source: Jay David, *The Life and Humor of Robin Williams*, p. 79.
227. Source: Bruce Laffey, *Beatrice Lillie*, p. 88.
228. Source: Art Linkletter, *I Didn't Do It Alone*, p. 88.

room and barley soup, noodle pudding, brisket, and so on (Totie says that this is what the Jewish Pilgrims ate). Because the refrigerator and freezer were already full, they carried the Thanksgiving food out to the garage and left it there, knowing that the weather was cold enough to keep the food safe. Thanksgiving morning they went to the garage, only to discover that a gardener had left the door to the garage open and a neighborhood dog had enjoyed the feast. For Thanksgiving, they ate in a restaurant, then drove around the neighborhood looking for a dog with heartburn.[229]

War

• Michael, the son of children's author Walter Dean Myers, served in the Persian Gulf War and came back to the United States safe and sound. About the experience of having a child serve as a soldier in a war, Mr. Myers says, "You hear this story about a woman waking up in the middle of the night in fear, and later she learns that her husband was killed at that exact moment. Well, that's a bunch of crap. The truth is, you wake up every night in fear. It was a very scary time."[230]

• One of Emma Washa's sons had an unenviable job during World War II. He worked in a hospital ward, and the wounded soldiers sometimes went crazy with pain and suffering. His job was to kneel on them to keep them from getting out of bed and hurting themselves. Later, this son died from a brain tumor. According to Ms. Washa, the brain tumor was caused by the insanity of war.[231]

Weddings

• In the first half of the 20th century, Edwin Porter was a preacher in Texas, where he performed many weddings. In those days, etiquette books said that $3 was the proper amount to pay the preacher for performing the wedding, but when asked what he was owed Rev. Porter simply answered, "Just pay me whatever you think your wife is worth." One new husband dug a quarter out of his pocket and asked if Rev. Porter had change! But another new husband dug into his pockets and hauled out bills, quarters, and other change, then he handed all his money to Rev. Porter without counting it, saying, "My wife is worth all I've got." (Because the marriage fees varied so widely, Rev. Porter's children made a game out of guessing the amount the groom would pay their father.)[232]

---

229. Source: Marilyn Hall and Rabbi Jerome Cutler, *The Celebrity Kosher Cookbook*, p. 35.

230. Source: Denise M. Jordan, *Walter Dean Myers: Writer for Real Teens*, p. 90.

231. Source: Jeanne Marie Laskas, *We Remember*, p. 95.

• In a Haverhill, Massachusetts, cemetery are several funeral stones dedicated to the wives of Captain Nathaniel Thurston. His final wife, who outlived him, is not there. During the good captain's final trip to the cemetery from Lansinburgh, New York, she rode beside his coffin in the undertaker's wagon while the undertaker and his son rode up front. On the way back home from the cemetery, she rode beside the undertaker up front while his son rode in back. When she and the undertaker returned back home to Lansinburgh, New York, they got married.[233]

• Aung San Suu Kyi of Burma fell in love with British citizen Michael Aris. In 1971, when he was working as a tutor in Bhutan for the royal family and she was working in New York City, she sent him 187 letters. They married even though Suu Kyi came from a prominent Burmese family and the Burmese people often are against intermarriage with foreigners. In fact, Chit Myaing, former Burmese ambassador to Great Britain, said, "The Burmese people would not like [Suu Kyi] marrying a foreigner. I knew that if I attended the wedding, I would be fired that day."[234]

• Frank Benson was the manager of a traveling Shakespearean troupe and a man who enjoyed sports. Once, he heard a rumor that one of his actors, Harold Large, was expected to ask a certain woman to marry him. Mr. Benson asked his wife, Constance, if she thought the woman would accept the marriage proposal. She replied, "I don't know. He hasn't made his fortune yet." This shocked Mr. Benson: "Good Heavens! I don't know what she wants—the fellow is one of the finest half-backs in England!"[235]

• One of Dini von Mueffling's best friends was Alison Gertz, who had contracted HIV, which developed into AIDS. Dini met a man, they fell in love, he asked her to marry him, and she accepted. However, Dini was worried about what Alison would say when she told her. She needn't have worried. After learning that the man, Richard, had asked Dini to marry him after knowing her for only three months, Alison asked, "What took him so long?"[236]

• Rabbi Shlomo Carlebach once wrote the wedding invitation for two of his friends, promising them, "It'll be the holiest wedding invitation in the world!" The invitation read, "The whole world is invited to the wedding of Ne'eman Rosen and Malka Gorman." The invitations were given out all through the

232. Source: Alyene Porter, *Papa was a Preacher*, pp. 106-107, 109.
233. Source: Robert E. Pike, *Granite Laughter and Marble Tears*, p. 63.
234. Source: Whitney Stewart, *Aung San Suu Kyi: Fearless Voice of Burma*, p. 53.
235. Source: Constance Benson, *Mainly Players*, p. 104.
236. Source: Michael Thomas Ford, *The Voices of AIDS*, pp. 64-65.

Haight-Ashbury district, and attending the wedding were many people whom Mr. Rosen and Ms. Gorman didn't know.[237]

• In the late 1890s and early 1900s, educated women were rare. For example, Ernestine Carey was educated in college at a time when few women were and those few were looked at somewhat strangely. When she married Frank B. Gilbreth, Jr., a newspaper reported, "Although a graduate of the University of California, the bride is nonetheless an extremely attractive young woman."[238]

• A woman walked into a fabric shop and asked for a fabric that would rustle when she walked. The proprietor found a suitable fabric for her, then out of curiosity asked what she wanted it for. The woman replied, "I am getting married to a blind man, and I want to make a wedding dress that rustles when I walk down the aisle so my fiancé will know when I've arrived at the altar."[239]

• Sonja Ely's five-year-old granddaughter was holding a wedding for two of her dolls. At one point, she spoke for the groom, saying to the minister, "Now you can read us our rights." Speaking for the minister, she then said, "You have the right to remain silent, anything you say can be held against you, you have the right to have an attorney present. You may kiss the bride."[240]

• In 1982, figure skater Dorothy Hamill married Dean Paul Martin, the son of entertainer Dean Martin. President Ronald Reagan was one of her neighbors at the time, but she didn't invite him to the wedding because she feared that the presence of the Secret Service guards would interfere with the wedding and with the enjoyment of the guests.[241]

• Tom Cahill used to be the coach of the Army football team. He played his college football at Niagara, where he was once caught sneaking into bed at 3 a.m. His punishment for breaking training was to copy the text of an entire book. He choose *Selecting a Mate in Marriage* and copied it from 9 p.m. to 7 a.m.[242]

• Richard Vaux, a Quaker, was secretary to a legation that appeared at the English court. He fit in well at court and wrote home that he had danced with Princess Victoria (who later became Queen of England). His mother read the letter, then remarked, "I do hope Richard won't marry out of meeting."[243]

237. Source: Yitta Halberstam Mandelbaum, *Holy Brother*, pp. 8-9.
238. Source: Frank B. Gilbreth, Jr. and Ernestine Gilbreth Carey, *Cheaper by the Dozen*, p. 36.
239. Source: Gerald Fuller, *Stories for All Seasons*, p. 65.
240. Source: Edward K. Rowell, editor, *Humor for Preaching and Teaching*, p. 183.
241. Source: William R. Sanford and Carl R. Green, *Dorothy Hamill*, pp. 29, 46.
242. Source: Gene Ward and Dick Hyman, *Football Wit and Humor*, p. 5.
243. Source: Irvin C. Poley and Ruth Verlenden Poley, *Friendly Anecdotes*, pp. 17-18.

• A Harvard football star was getting married. As he knelt before the bishop, the guests started laughing. The ushers—all of whom were football fans—had printed on the sole of his left shoe "TO HELL" and on the sole of his right shoe "WITH YALE."[244]

Widows

• Dipa Ma started studying meditation after she fell into a deep depression after the sudden death of her husband, which followed the deaths of two of her children. She asked herself, "What can I take with me when I die?" Looking around, she saw many material possessions and her daughter, but nothing she could take with her when she died. She then thought, "Let me go to the meditation center. Maybe I can find something there I can take with me when I die." In meditation, she found peace.[245]

• Women of the west gained respect from men of the west. After a widow travelling west succeeded through sheer determination in getting her children alive through Death Valley, the men traveling with her agreed that "she was the best man of the party."[246]

Work

• Aryeh Labe, aka Archie Lionel, was the youngest brother of the mother of Al Capp, creator of the comic strip *Li'l Abner*. As a young man, he didn't know whether to become a Rabbi or a dancer. One day, Aryeh and two friends visited his sister's family. After eating, the two friends put on a dance demonstration for the family. They were magnificent, and Al's mother asked her brother, "Archie, *kind*, can you dance that way?" Archie replied, "Never in a million years." Hearing that, she advised her brother, "Then, Archie, *tierer*, become a Rabbi." He did. (By the way, the friends really were magnificent dancers. Their names were Arthur and Katherine Murray.)[247]

• Pulitzer Prize-winning reporter Meyer Berger was very poor when he was growing up. As a child, he and two brothers—one older, one younger—got up early to sell newspapers in diners. After the first batch of newspapers was sold, the youngest brother quit working; after the second batch was sold, Meyer quit working; finally, after all the newspapers were sold, the oldest brother quit working. As

244. Source: Gene Ward and Dick Hyman, *Football Wit and Humor*, p. 83.
245. Source: Sharon Salzberg, *A Heart as Wide as the World*, pp. 10-11.
246. Source: Brandon Marie Miller, *Buffalo Gals: Women of the Old West*, p. 19.
247. Source: Elliott Caplin, *Al Capp Remembered*, pp. 14-15.

an adult, Meyer would sometimes arrive at work carrying a dozen copies of the same newspaper—he never said no to a newsboy.[248]

• While appearing as a lecturer across the country, Will Rogers included a comic bit in which he and his nephew moved a piano across the stage. The nephew did the hard work of moving the piano, while Will "helped" by moving the piano stool. One night, an accident occurred on stage. The piano collapsed, the audience laughed, and Will said later, "I wish it would happen every night."[249]

• Eugene Field wanted a raise while he was working for the *Chicago Daily News*. So one day he and his four small children dressed in rags and went inside the editor's office, where the children begged, "Please, sir, won't you raise our father's wages?"[250]

248. Source: Mildred and Milton Lewis, *Famous Modern Newspaper Writers*, p. 32.
249. Source: Mary Malone, *Will Rogers: Cowboy Philosopher*, p. 81.
250. Source: H. Allen Smith, *The Compleat Practical Joker*, p. 258.

Bibliography for 250 Anecdotes About Religion

Aaseng, Rolf E. *Anyone Can Teach (they said)*. Minneapolis, Minnesota: Augsburg Publishing House, 1965.

Adams, Joey. *The Borscht Belt*. With Henry Tobias. New York: Avon Books, 1966.

Adams, Joey. *The God Bit*. Boston, Massachusetts: G.K. Hall & Co., 1975.

Adler, Bill. *Jewish Wit and Wisdom*. New York: Dell Publishing Co, Inc, 1969.

Aflaki, Shams al-Din Ahmad. *Legends of the Sufis: Selected Anecdotes from the Work Entitled, The Acts of the Adepts by Shemsu-'D-Din Ahmed, El Eflaki*. London: Theosophical Publishing House, 1976.

Alley, Ken. *Awkward Christian Soldiers*. Wheaton, Illinois: Harold Shaw Publishers, 1998.

Benson, Constance. *Mainly Players: Bensonian Memories*. London: Thornton Butterworth, Ltd., 1926.

Berger, Phil. *The Last Laugh: The World of the Stand-Up Comics*. New York: William Morris and Co., Inc., 1975.

Besserman, Perle and Manfred Steger. *Crazy Clouds: Zen Radicals, Rebels, and Reformers*. Boston: Shambala, 1991.

Blackman, Sushila, compiler and editor. *Graceful Exits: How Great Beings Die*. New York: Weatherhill, Inc., 1997.

Bono, Chastity. *Family Outing*. With Billie Fitzpatrick. Boston: Little, Brown and Company, 1998.

Bourke, Dale Hanson. *Everyday Miracles: Holy Moments in a Mother's Day.* Dallas: Word Publishing, 1989.

Boxer, Tim. *The Jewish Celebrity Hall of Fame.* New York: Shapolsky Publishers, 1987.

Brown, Cordell. *I am What I am by the Grace of God.* Warsaw, Ohio: Echoing Hills Village Foundation, 1996.

Buber, Martin. *The Way of Man: According to the Teaching of Hasidism.* New York: The Citadel Press, 1966.

Burke, John. *Rogue's Progress: The Fabulous Adventures of Wilson Mizner.* New York: G.P. Putnam's Sons, 1975.

Butz, Geneva M. *Christmas in All Seasons.* Cleveland, OH: United Church Press, 1995.

Cantor, Eddie. *Take My Life.* Written with Jane Kesner Ardmore. Garden City, New York, 1957.

Carter, Judy. *The Homo Handbook.* New York: Fireside Books, 1996.

Chappell, Helen. *The Chesapeake Book of the Dead: Tombstones, Epitaphs, Histories, Reflections, and Oddments of the Region.* Baltimore, Maryland: The Johns Hopkins University Press, 1999.

Charles, Helen White, collector and editor. *Quaker Chuckles and Other True Stories About Friends.* Oxford, OH: H.W. Charles, 1961.

Chesto, Kathleen O'Connell. *Why Are the Dandelions Weeds?* Kansas City, MO: Sheed & Ward, 1993.

Cleary, Thomas, translator. *Zen Antics: A Hundred Stories of Enlightenment.* Boston: Shambhala Publications, Inc., 1993.

Clemens, Cyril, editor. *Mark Twain Anecdotes.* Webster Groves, Mo.: Mark Twain Society, 1929.

Clemens, Cyril. "Mark Twain's Religion." Webster Groves, Missouri: International Mark Twain Society, 1935.

Clinton, Kate. *Don't Get Me Started.* New York: Ballantine Books, 1998.

Clower, Jerry. *Let the Hammer Down!* With Gerry Wood. Waco, Texas: Word Books, Publisher, 1979.

Clower, Jerry. *Life Everlaughter: The Heart and Humor of Jerry Clower.* Nashville, Tennessee: Rutledge Hill Press, 1987.

Collins, Beulah, collector. *For Benefit of Clergy.* New York: Grosset & Dunlap, 1966.

Deedy, John. *A Book of Catholic Anecdotes.* Allen, Texas: Thomas More, 1997.

Dosick, Wayne. *Golden Rules: The Ten Ethical Rules Parents Need to Teach Their Children.* San Francisco: HarperSanFrancisco, 1995.

Downing, Charles. *Tales of the Hodja.* New York: Henry Z. Walck, Inc., 1965.

Edwards, Susan. *Erma Bombeck: A Life in Humor.* New York: Avon Books, 1997.

Epstein, Lawrence J. *A Treasury of Jewish Anecdotes.* Northvale, New Jersey: Jason Aronson, Inc., 1989.

Evans, J. Edward. *Freedom of Religion.* Minneapolis, MN: Lerner Publications Company, 1990.

Fadiman, James and Robert Frager. *Essential Sufism.* San Francisco: HarperSanFrancisco, 1997.

Fager, Chuck. *Quakers are Funny! A New Collection of Quaker Humor.* Falls Church, VA: Kimo Press, 1987.

Farzan, Massud. *Another Way of Laughter: A Collection of Sufi Humor.* New York: E.P. Dutton & Co., Inc., 1973.

Fecher, Msgr. Vincent. *"The Lord and I": Vignettes from the Life of a Parish Priest.* New York: Alba House, 1990.

Fesquet, Henri, collector. *Wit and Wisdom of Good Pope John.* Translated by Salvator Attanasio. New York: P.J. Kenedy & Sons, 1964.

Finck, Henry T. *Musical Laughs.* New York: Funk & Wagnalls Company, 1924.

Fonteyn, Margot. *Autobiography*. New York: Alfred A. Knopf, 1976.

Ford, Michael Thomas. *Outspoken: Role Models from the Lesbian and Gay Community*. New York: Morrow Junior Books, 1998.

Foster, Leila Merrell. *Benjamin Franklin: Founding Father and Inventor*. Springfield, NJ: Enslow Publications, Inc., 1997.

Freeman, Dorothy Rhodes. *St. Patrick's Day*. Berkeley Heights, NJ: Enslow Publications, Inc., 1992.

Fuller, Gerald. *Stories for All Seasons*. Mystic, CT: Twenty-Third Publications, 1996.

Garagiola, Joe. *It's Anybody's Ballgame*. New York: Jove Books, 1988.

Garvey, Reverend Francis J. *Favorite Humor of Famous Americans*. Kandiyohi, Minnesota: Reverend Francis J. Garvey, 1981.

Gershick, Zsa Zsa. *Gay Old Girls*. Los Angeles: Alyson Books, 1998.

Glatzer, Nahum N., editor. *Hammer on the Rock: A Short Midrash Reader*. Translated by Jacob Sloan. New York: Schocken Books, 1962.

Glenn, Menahem G. *Israel Salanter: Religious-Ethical Thinker*. New York: Bloch Publishing Company, 1953.

Goldwasser, Rabbi Dovid. *It Happened in Heaven: Personal Stories of Inspiration*. Jerusalem: Feldheim Publishers, 1995.

González-Balado, José Luis, compiler. *Mother Teresa: In My Own Words*. New York: Gramercy Books, 1996.

Goodman, Philip. *Rejoice in Thy Festival*. New York: Bloch Publishing Company, 1956.

Gorman, Tom, and Jerome Holtzman. *Three and Two!* New York: Charles Scribner's Sons, 1979.

Henry, Lewis C. *Humorous Anecdotes About Famous People*. Garden City, New York: Halcyon House, 1948.

Himelstein, Shmuel. *A Touch of Wisdom, A Touch of Wit*. Brooklyn, New York: Mesorah Publications, Limited, 1991.

Himelstein, Shmuel. *Words of Wisdom, Words of Wit*. Brooklyn, New York: Mesorah Publications, Ltd., 1993.

Holloway, Gary. *Saints, Demons, and Asses: Southern Preacher Anecdotes*. Bloomington, Indiana: Indiana University Press, 1989.

Hope, Bob. *The Road to Hollywood: My Forty-Year Love Affair With the Movies*. With Bob Thomas. Garden City, New York: Doubleday & Company, Inc., 1977.

Hyman, Dick. *Potomac Wind and Wisdom: Jokes, Lies, and True Stories By and About America's Politics and Politicians*. Brattleboro, Vermont: The Stephen Greene Press, 1980.

Jacobs, J. Vernon, compiler. *450 True Stories from Church History*. Grand Rapids, Michigan: Wm. B. Eerdmans Publishing Company, 1955.

Kennedy, Robert E. *Zen Spirit, Christian Spirit: The Place of Zen in Christian Life*. New York: Continuum Publishing Company, 1995.

Klare, Roger. *Gregor Mendel: Father of Genetics*. Springfield, NJ: Enslow Publications, Inc., 1997.

Klinger, Kurt, collector. *A Pope Laughs: Stories of John XXIII*. Translated by Sally McDevitt Cunneen. New York: Holt, Rinehart and Winston, 1964.

Kolasky, John, collector and compiler. *Look, Comrade—The People are Laughing....* Toronto, Ontario: Peter Martin Associates Limited, 1972.

Kornfield, Jack, and Christina Feldman. *Soul Food: Stories to Nourish the Spirit and the Heart*. San Francisco: HarperSanFrancisco, 1996. This is a revised edition of their 1991 book *Stories of the Spirit, Stories of the Heart*.

Linkletter, Art. *I Didn't Do It Alone: The Autobiography of Art Linkletter*. Ottawa, Illinois: Caroline House Publishers, Inc., 1980.

Linkletter, Art. *Kids Say the Darndest Things!* New York: Bonanza Books, 1978.

Lipman, Steve. *Laughter in Hell: The Use of Humor during the Holocaust*. Northvale, New Jersey: Jason Aronson Inc., 1991.

Lyman, Darryl. *Holocaust Rescuers: Ten Stories of Courage*. Springfield, NJ: Enslow Publications, Inc., 1999.

Mandelbaum, Yitta Halberstam. *Holy Brother: Inspiring Stories and Enchanted Tales About Rabbi Shlomo Carlebach*. Northvale, New Jersey: Jason Aronson Inc., 1997.

Marx, Arthur. *Life With Groucho*. New York: Simon and Schuster, 1954.

Marx, Groucho. *Groucho and Me*. New York: Bernard Geis Associates, 1959.

Maverick, Jr., Maury. *Texas Iconoclast*. Edited by Allan O. Kownslar. Fort Worth, Texas, Texas: Texas Christian University Press, 1997.

McCormick, Anita Louise. *Native Americans and the Reservation in American History*. Springfield, NJ: Enslow Publications, Inc., 1996.

McNey, Martha. *Leslie's Story*. Minneapolis, MN: Lerner Publications Company, 1996.

Mendelsohn, S. Felix. *Here's a Good One: Stories of Jewish Wit and Wisdom*. New York: Block Publishing Co., 1947.

Metil, Luana, and Jace Townsend. *The Story of Karate: From Buddhism to Bruce Lee*. Minneapolis, MN: Lerner Publications Company, 1995.

Michaels, Louis. *The Humor and Warmth of Pope John XXIII: His Anecdotes and Legends*. New York: Pocket Books, Inc., 1965.

Mindess, Harvey. *The Chosen People? A Testament, Both Old and New, to the Therapeutic Power of Jewish Wit and Humor*. Los Angeles: Nash Publishing Corporation, 1972.

Mingo, Jack. *The Juicy Parts*. New York: The Berkley Publishing Group, 1996.

Moody, Ivy. *Illustrations with a Point*. Cincinnati, Ohio: The Standard Publishing Company, 1961.

Mostel, Kate, and Madeline Gilford. *170 Years of Show Business*. With Jack Gilford and Zero Mostel. New York: Random House, 1978.

Nardo, Don. *The Trial of Joan of Arc*. San Diego, CA: Lucent Books, 1998.

Parker, John F. *"If Elected, I Promise…."* Garden City, New York: Doubleday & Co., Inc., 1960.

Pellowski, Michael J. *Baseball's Funniest People*. New York: Sterling Publishing Co., 1997.

Petuchowski, Jakob J., translator and editor. *Our Masters Taught: Rabbinic Stories and Sayings*. New York: Crossroad, 1982.

Phares, Ross. *Bible in Pocket, Gun in Hand: The Story of Frontier Religion*. Garden City, New York: Doubleday & Company, Inc., 1964.

Poley, Irvin C., and Ruth Verlenden Poley. *Friendly Anecdotes*. New York: Harper & Brothers, Publishers, 1950.

Porter, Alyene. *Papa was a Preacher*. New York: Abingdon Press, 1944.

Powers, Tom. *Steven Spielberg: Master Storyteller*. Minneapolis, MN: Lerner Publications Company, 1997.

Reps, Paul, compiler. *Zen Flesh, Zen Bones*. Rutland, Vermont: Charles E. Tuttle Co., 1957.

Rowell, Edward K., editor. *Humor for Preaching and Teaching*. Grand Rapids, Michigan: Baker Books, 1996.

Russell, Fred. *I'll Try Anything Twice*. Nashville, Tennessee: The McQuiddy Press, 1945.

Ruth, Amy. *Mother Teresa*. Minneapolis, MN: Lerner Publications Company, 1999.

Salkin, Jeffrey K. *Being God's Partner: How to Find the Hidden Link Between Spirituality and Your Work*. Woodstock, Vermont: Jewish Lights Publishing, 1994.

Salzberg, Sharon. *A Heart as Wide as the World: Stories on the Path to Lovingkindness*. Boston, Massachusetts: Shambhala Publications, Inc., 1997.

Salzberg, Sharon. *Lovingkindness: The Revolutionary Art of Happiness*. Boston: Shambala Publications, Inc., 1995.

Samra, Cal and Rose, editors. *Holy Hilarity*. Colorado Springs, Colorado: Water-Brook Press, 1999.

Samra, Cal and Rose, editors. *Holy Humor*. Colorado Springs, Colorado: Water-Brook Press, 1997.

Schraff, Anne. *Women of Peace: Nobel Peace Prize Winners*. Hillside, NJ: Enslow Publications, Inc., 1994.

Schuman, Michael A. *Martin Luther King: Leader for Civil Rights*. Springfield, NJ: Enslow Publications, Inc., 1996.

Sessions, William H., collector. *Laughter in Quaker Grey*. York, England: William Sessions Limited, 1966.

Sessions, William H., collector. *More Quaker Laughter*. York, England: William Sessions Limited, 1974.

Sherrow, Victoria. *The Righteous Gentiles*. San Diego, CA: Lucent Books. 1998.

Silverman, William B. *Rabbinic Wisdom and Jewish Values*. New York: Union of American Hebrew Congregations, 1971.

Smith, H. Allen. *The Compleat Practical Joker*. Garden City, New York: Doubleday and Company, Inc., 1953.

Smith, H. Allen. *People Named Smith*. Garden City, New York: Doubleday & Company, Inc., 1950.

Snead, Sam. *The Game I Love: Wisdom, Insight, and Instruction from Golf's Greatest Player*. With Fran Pirozzolo. New York: Ballantine Books, 1997.

Spalding, Henry D. *Jewish Laffs*. Middle Village, New York: Jonathan David Publishers, Inc., 1982.

Stewart, Whitney. *The 14th Dalai Lama: Spiritual Leader of Tibet.* Minneapolis, MN: Lerner Publications Company. 1996.

Stryk, Lucien and Takashi Ikemoto, selectors and translators. *Zen: Poems, Prayers, Sermons, Anecdotes, Interviews.* Chicago: Swallow Press, 1981.

Taylor, Glenhall. *Before Television: The Radio Years.* New York: A.S. Barnes and Company, 1979.

Telushkin, Rabbi Joseph. *Jewish Humor: What the Best Jewish Jokes Say About the Jews.* New York: William Morrow and Company, 1992.

Telushkin, Rabbi Joseph. *Jewish Wisdom: Ethical, Spiritual, and Historical Lessons from the Great Works and Thinkers.* New York: William Morrow and Company, Inc., 1994.

Thomas, Bob. *Bud & Lou: The Abbott and Costello Story.* Philadelphia: J.B. Lippincott Company, 1977.

Thompson, Joe. *Growing Up with "Shoeless Joe."* Greenville, SC: Burgess International, 1997.

Tsai, Chih-Chung (editor and illustrator) and Kok Kok Kiang (translator). *The Book of Zen.* Singapore: Asiapac, 1990.

Tsai, Chih-Chung. *Zen Speaks: Shouts of Nothingness.* New York: Anchor Books, 1994.

Tully, Jim. *A Dozen and One.* Hollywood: Murray & Gee, Inc., Publishers, 1943.

Udall, Morris K. *Too Funny to be President.* With Bob Neuman and Randy Udall. New York: Henry Holt and Company, 1988.

Unsworth, Tim. *Here Comes Everybody! Stories of Church.* New York: The Crossroad Publishing Company, 1993.

Van Dyke, Dick. *Faith, Hope and Hilarity.* Edited by Ray Parker. Garden City, New York: Doubleday and Company, Inc, 1970.

Voskressenski, Alexei D., compiler and editor. *Cranks, Knaves, and Jokers of the Celestial.* Translated from the Chinese by Alexei Voskressenski and Vladimir Larin. Commack, NY: Nova Science Publishers, Inc., 1997.

Wagenknecht, Edward. *Merely Players.* Norman, OK: University of Oklahoma Press, 1966.

Ward, Hiley H., editor. *Ecumania: The Humor That Happens When Catholics, Jews, and Protestants Come Together.* New York: Association Press, 1968.

Weston, Anthony. *A Practical Companion to Ethics.* New York: Oxford University Press, 1997.

Wiesel, Elie. *Souls on Fire: Portraits and Legends of Hasidic Masters.* Translated from the French by Marion Wiesel. New York: Random House, 1972.

Wise, Stephen S. *How to Face Life.* New York: B.W. Huebsch, 1917.

Woughter, William. *All Preachers of Our God & King.* Wheaton, Illinois: Harold Shaw Publishers, 1997.

Zall, P.M. *George Washington Laughing: Humorous Anecdotes by and about our first President from Original Sources.* Hamden, Conn: Archon Books, 1989.

Bibliography for 250 Anecdotes About Family

Aaseng, Rolf E. *Anyone Can Teach (they said)*. Minneapolis, Minnesota: Augsburg Publishing House, 1965.

Adler, Bill. *The Letterman Wit: His Life and Humor*. New York: Carroll & Graf Publishers, Inc., 1994.

Adler, Bill, and Bruce Cassiday. *The World of Jay Leno: His Humor and His Life*. New York: Carol Publishing Group, 1992.

Alda, Frances. *Men, Women, and Tenors*. Boston: Houghton Mifflin Company, 1937.

Alley, Ken. *Awkward Christian Soldiers*. Wheaton, Illinois: Harold Shaw Publishers, 1998.

Arden, Eve. *Three Phases of Eve: An Autobiography*. New York: St. Martin's Press, 1985.

Barnhouse, Donald Grey. *Let Me Illustrate: Stories, Anecdotes, Illustrations*. Westwood, New Jersey: Fleming H. Revell Company, 1967.

Benson, Constance. *Mainly Players: Bensonian Memories*. London: Thornton Butterworth, Ltd., 1926.

Berger, Phil. *The Last Laugh: The World of the Stand-Up Comics*. New York: William Morris and Co., Inc., 1975.

Bernard, André. *Now All We Need is a Title: Famous Book Titles and How They Got That Way*. New York: W.W. Norton & Company, 1995.

Blumberg, Arthur, and Phyllis Blumberg. *The Unwritten Curriculum: Things Learned But Not Taught in Schools.* Thousand Oaks, CA: Corwin Press, Inc., 1994.

Bombeck, Erma. *I Want to Grow Hair, I Want to Grow Up, I Want to Go to Boise.* New York: Harper and Row, Publishers, 1989.

Bono, Chastity. *Family Outing.* With Billie Fitzpatrick. Boston: Little, Brown and Company, 1998.

Bourke, Dale Hanson. *Everyday Miracles: Holy Moments in a Mother's Day.* Dallas: Word Publishing, 1989.

Boxer, Tim. *The Jewish Celebrity Hall of Fame.* New York: Shapolsky Publishers, 1987.

Brady, Logan Munger. *Amusing Anecdotes: Humorous Stories With a Moral.* Ann Arbor, Michigan: Ann Arbor Book Company, 1993.

Brennan, Christine. *Inside Edge: A Revealing Journey into the Secret World of Figure Skating.* New York: Scribner, 1996.

Brown, Cordell. *I am What I am by the Grace of God.* Warsaw, Ohio: Echoing Hills Village Foundation, 1996.

Brown, Joe E. *Laughter is a Wonderful Thing.* As told to Ralph Hancock. New York: A.S. Barnes and Co., 1956.

Bryan III, J. *Merry Gentlemen (and One Lady).* New York: Atheneum, 1985.

Burchard, S.H. *Dorothy Hamill.* New York: Harcourt Brace Jovanovich, 1978.

Burke, John. *Rogue's Progress: The Fabulous Adventures of Wilson Mizner.* New York: G.P. Putnam's Sons, 1975.

Campbell, Archie. *Archie Campbell: An Autobiography.* With Ben Bryd. Memphis, TN: Memphis State University Press, 1981.

Cantor, Eddie. *The Way I See It.* Englewood Cliffs, New Jersey: 1959.

Caplin, Elliott. *Al Capp Remembered.* Bowling Green, OH: Bowling Green State University Popular Press, 1994.

Carpenter, Angelica Shirley, and Jean Shirley. *Frances Hodgson Burnett: Beyond the Secret Garden*. Minneapolis, MN: Lerner Publications Company, 1990.

Carter, Judy. *The Homo Handbook*. New York: Fireside Books, 1996.

Charles, Helen White, collector and editor. *Quaker Chuckles and Other True Stories About Friends*. Oxford, OH: H.W. Charles, 1961.

Châtaigneau, Gérard, and Steve Milton. *Figure Skating Now: Olympic and World Stars*. Willowdale, Ontario, Canada: Firefly Books, 2001.

Chenevière, Alain. *Maud in France*. Minneapolis, MN: Lerner Publications Company, 1996.

Clemens, Cyril, editor. *Mark Twain Anecdotes*. Webster Groves, Mo.: Mark Twain Society, 1929.

Clinton, Kate. *Don't Get Me Started*. New York: Ballantine Books, 1998.

Clower, Jerry. *Life Everlaughter: The Heart and Humor of Jerry Clower*. Nashville, Tennessee: Rutledge Hill Press, 1987.

Conner, Bart. *Winning the Gold*. With Coach Paul Ziert. New York: Warner Books, Inc., 1985.

David, Jay. *The Life and Humor of Robin Williams*. New York: William Morrow and Company, Inc., 1999.

DeCaro, Frank. *A Boy Named Phyllis*. New York: Viking, 1996.

Dole, Bob. *Great Political Wit*. New York: Doubleday, 1998.

Dosick, Wayne. *Golden Rules: The Ten Ethical Rules Parents Need to Teach Their Children*. San Francisco: HarperSanFrancisco, 1995.

Drennan, Robert E., editor. *The Algonquin Wits*. New York: The Citadel Press, 1968.

Edwards, Susan. *Erma Bombeck: A Life in Humor*. New York: Avon Books, 1997.

Epstein, Lawrence J. *A Treasury of Jewish Anecdotes*. Northvale, New Jersey: Jason Aronson, Inc., 1989.

Ewen, David, complier. *Listen to the Mocking Words*. New York: Arco Publishing Co., 1945.

Fadiman, James, and Robert Frager. *Essential Sufism*. San Francisco: HarperSan-Francisco, 1997.

Farrell, Suzanne. *Holding On to the Air*. New York: Summit Books, 1990.

Feinberg, Morris "Moe." *Larry: The Stooge in the Middle*. With G.P. Skratz. San Francisco: Last Gasp of San Francisco, 1984.

Ford, Carin T. *Legends of American Dance and Choreography*. Berkeley Heights, NJ: Enslow Publications, Inc., 2000.

Ford, Michael Thomas. *The Voices of AIDS: Twelve Unforgettable People Talk About How AIDS has Changed Their Lives*. New York: Morrow Junior Books, 1995.

Fox, Grace. *Everyday Etiquette*. Garden City, New York: Doubleday Direct, Inc., 1996.

Frank, Rusty E. *Tap! The Greatest Tap Dance Stars and Their Stories, 1900-1955*. New York: William Morrow and Company, Inc., 1990.

Franks, A.H., editor. *Pavlova: A Collection of Memoirs*. New York: Da Capo Press, Inc., 1956.

Fuller, Gerald. *Stories for All Seasons*. Mystic, CT: Twenty-Third Publications, 1996.

Gallo, Hank. *Comedy Explosion: A New Generation*. Photographs by Ed Edahl. New York: Thunder's Mouth Press, 1991.

Garagiola, Joe. *It's Anybody's Ballgame*. New York: Jove Books, 1988.

Gershick, Zsa Zsa. *Gay Old Girls*. Los Angeles: Alyson Books, 1998.

Gilbreth, Jr., Frank B. and Ernestine Gilbreth Carey. *Cheaper by the Dozen*. New York: Thomas Y. Crowell Company, 1948.

Gleasner, Diana C. *Track and Field*. New York: Harvey House, Publishers, 1977.

Gonzales, Doreen. *Diego Rivera: His Art, His Life.* Berkeley Heights, NJ: Enslow Publications, Inc., 1996.

Gordeeva, Ekaterina. *My Sergei: A Love Story.* With E.M. Swift. New York: Warner Books, Inc., 1996.

Greenberg, Keith Elliot. *Zack's Story.* Minneapolis, MN: Lerner Publications Company, 1996.

Grenfell, Joyce. *Joyce Grenfell Requests the Pleasure.* London: Macdonald Futura Publishers Ltd., 1976.

Guernsey, JoAnn Bren. *Tipper Gore: Voice for the Voiceless.* Minneapolis, MN: Lerner Publications Company, 1994.

Hall, Marilyn, and Rabbi Jerome Cutler. *The Celebrity Kosher Cookbook.* Los Angeles: J.P. Tarcher, Inc., 1975.

Henry, Lewis C. *Humorous Anecdotes About Famous People.* Garden City, New York: Halcyon House, 1948.

Hill, Christine M. *Ten Terrific Authors for Teens.* Berkeley Heights, NJ: Enslow Publications, Inc., 2000.

Himelstein, Shmuel. *A Touch of Wisdom, A Touch of Wit.* Brooklyn, New York: Mesorah Publications, Limited, 1991.

Himelstein, Shmuel. *Words of Wisdom, Words of Wit.* Brooklyn, New York: Mesorah Publications, Ltd., 1993.

Howard, Megan. *Madeleine Albright.* Minneapolis, MN: Lerner Publications Company, 1999.

Jacobs, Linda. *Mary Decker: Speed Records and Spaghetti.* St. Paul, MN: EMI Corporation, 1975.

Jordan, Denise M. *Walter Dean Myers: Writer for Real Teens.* Berkeley Heights, NJ: Enslow Publications, Inc., 1999.

Josephson, Judith Pinkerton. *Nikki Giovanni: Poet of the People.* Berkeley Heights, NJ: Enslow Publications, Inc., 2000.

Kandel, Bethany. *Trevor's Story*. Minneapolis, MN: Lerner Publications Company, 1997.

Kanner, Bernice. *The 100 Best TV Commercials...and Why They Worked*. New York: Times Books, 1999.

Karolyi, Bela, and Nancy Ann Richardson. *Feel No Fear: The Power, Passion, and Politics of a Life in Gymnastics*. New York: Hyperion, 1994.

Kistler, Darci. *Ballerina: My Story*. With Alicia Kistler. New York: Pocket Books, Inc., 1993.

Klinger, Kurt, collector. *A Pope Laughs: Stories of John XXIII*. Translated by Sally McDevitt Cunneen. New York: Holt, Rinehart and Winston, 1964.

Kramer, Barbara. *John Glenn: A Space Biography*. Springfield, NJ: Enslow Publications, Inc., 1998.

Laffey, Bruce. *Beatrice Lillie: The Funniest Woman in the World*. New York: Wynwood Press, 1989.

Laskas, Jeanne Marie. *We Remember: Women Born at the Turn of the Century Tell the Stories of Their Lives*. Photographs by Lynn Johnson. New York: William Morrow and Company, 1999.

Lewis, Mildred and Milton. *Famous Modern Newspaper Writers*. New York: Dodd, Mead & Company, 1962.

Linkletter, Art. *I Didn't Do It Alone: The Autobiography of Art Linkletter*. Ottawa, Illinois: Caroline House Publishers, Inc., 1980.

Linkletter, Art. *Oops! Or, Life's Awful Moments*. Garden City, New York: Doubleday & Company, Inc., 1967.

Lipinski, Tara, and Emily Costello. *Tara Lipinski: Triumph on Ice*. New York: Bantam Books, 1997.

Madison, Bob. *American Horror Writers*. Berkeley Heights, NJ: Enslow Publications, Inc., 2001.

Malone, Mary. *Will Rogers: Cowboy Philosopher*. Springfield, NJ: Enslow Publications, Inc., 1996.

Mandelbaum, Yitta Halberstam. *Holy Brother: Inspiring Stories and Enchanted Tales About Rabbi Shlomo Carlebach*. Northvale, New Jersey: Jason Aronson, Inc., 1997.

Marx, Arthur. *Life With Groucho*. New York: Simon and Schuster, 1954.

Maverick, Jr., Maury. *Texas Iconoclast*. Edited by Allan O. Kownslar. Fort Worth, Texas, Texas: Texas Christian University Press, 1997.

McCann, Sean, compiler. *The Wit of the Irish*. Nashville, Tenn.: Aurora Publishers, Ltd., 1970.

Michaels, Louis. *The Humor and Warmth of Pope John XXIII: His Anecdotes and Legends*. New York: Pocket Books, Inc., 1965.

Miller, Brandon Marie. *Buffalo Gals: Women of the Old West*. Minneapolis, MN: Lerner Publications Company, 1995.

Miller, Claudia. *Shannon Miller: My Child, My Hero*. Norman, Oklahoma: University of Oklahoma Press, 1999.

Mindess, Harvey. *The Chosen People? A Testament, Both Old and New, to the Therapeutic Power of Jewish Wit and Humor*. Los Angeles: Nash Publishing Corporation, 1972.

Mockridge, Norton. *A Funny Thing Happened....* Greenwich, CT: Fawcett Publications, Inc., 1966.

Morgan, Henry. *Here's Morgan!* New York: Barricade Books, Inc., 1994.

Morley, Robert. *Around the World in Eighty-One Years*. London: Hodder & Stoughton, 1990.

Mostel, Kate, and Madeline Gilford. *170 Years of Show Business*. With Jack Gilford and Zero Mostel. New York: Random House, 1978.

Northrup, Mary. *American Computer Pioneers*. Springfield, NJ: Enslow Publications, Inc., 1998.

Pike, Robert E. *Granite Laughter and Marble Tears.* Brattleboro, VT: Stephen Daye Press, 1938.

Poley, Irvin C., and Ruth Verlenden Poley. *Friendly Anecdotes.* New York: Harper & Brothers, Publishers, 1950.

Porter, Alyene. *Papa was a Preacher.* New York: Abingdon Press, 1944.

Roessel, Monty. *Kinaaldá: A Navajo Girl Grows Up.* Minneapolis, MN: Lerner Publications Company, 1993.

Rogers, Fred. *Dear Mister Rogers, Does It Ever Rain in Your Neighborhood? Letters to Mister Rogers.* New York: Penguin Books, 1996.

Rogers, Fred. *You Are Special.* New York: Viking, 1994.

Rowell, Edward K., editor. *Humor for Preaching and Teaching.* Grand Rapids, Michigan: Baker Books, 1996.

Salzberg, Sharon. *A Heart as Wide as the World: Stories on the Path to Lovingkindness.* Boston, Massachusetts: Shambhala Publications, Inc., 1997.

Samra, Cal and Rose, editors. *More Holy Hilarity.* Colorado Springs, Colorado: WaterBrook Press, 1999.

Sanford, William R., and Carl R. Green. *Dorothy Hamill.* New York: Crestwood House, 1993.

Schafer, Kermit. *All Time Great Bloopers.* New York: Avenel Books, 1973.

Schafer, Kermit. *Best of Bloopers.* New York: Avenel Books, 1973.

Schraff, Anne. *Ralph Bunche: Winner of the Nobel Peace Prize.* Berkeley Heights, NJ: Enslow Publications, Inc., 1999.

Schulman, Arlene. *Carmine's Story.* Minneapolis, MN: Lerner Publications Company, 1997.

Sessions, William H., collector. *Laughter in Quaker Grey.* York, England: William Sessions Limited, 1966.

Sessions, William H., collector. *More Quaker Laughter.* York, England: William Sessions Limited, 1974.

Shawn, Ted. *One Thousand and One Night Stands.* With Gray Poole. New York: Da Capo Press, Inc., 1979.

Slezak, Leo. *Song of Motley.* New York: Arno Press, 1977.

Smith, Bob. *Openly Bob.* New York: William Morrow and Company, Inc., 1997.

Smith, H. Allen. *The Compleat Practical Joker.* Garden City, New York: Doubleday and Company, Inc., 1953.

Stewart, Whitney. *Aung San Suu Kyi: Fearless Voice of Burma.* Minneapolis, MN: Lerner Publications Company, 1997.

Strug, Kerri. *Landing on My Feet: A Diary of Dreams.* With John P. Lopez. Kansas City, Missouri: Andrews McMeel Publishing, 1997.

Taylor, Robert Lewis. *W.C. Fields: His Follies and Fortunes.* Garden City, New York: Doubleday and Company, Inc., 1949.

Telushkin, Rabbi Joseph. *Jewish Wisdom: Ethical, Spiritual, and Historical Lessons from the Great Works and Thinkers.* New York: William Morrow and Company, Inc., 1994.

Tobias, Andrew. *The Best Little Boy in the World Grows Up.* New York: Random House, 1998.

Ward, Gene and Dick Hyman, collectors. *Football Wit and Humor.* New York: Grosset & Dunlap, Publishers, 1970.

Watson, Richard. *The Philosopher's Diet: How to Lose Weight and Change the World.* Boston: The Atlantic Monthly Press, 1985.

Williams, Kenneth. *Acid Drops.* London: J.M. Dent & Sons, Ltd., 1980.

Willson, Meredith. *And There I Stood With My Piccolo.* Westport, CT: Greenwood Press, Publishers, 1948.

Woughter, William. *All Preachers of Our God & King.* Wheaton, Illinois: Harold Shaw Publishers, 1997.

Youngman, Henny. *Take My Life, Please!* With Neal Karlen. New York: William Morris and Company, Inc., 1991.

About the Author

It was a dark and stormy night. Suddenly a cry rang out, and on a hot summer night in 1954, Josephine, wife of Carl Bruce, gave birth to a boy—me. Unfortunately, this young married couple allowed Reuben Saturday, Josephine's brother, to name their first-born. Reuben, aka "The Joker," decided that Bruce was a nice name, so he decided to name me Bruce Bruce. I have gone by my middle name—David—ever since.

Being named Bruce David Bruce hasn't been all bad. Bank tellers remember me very quickly, so I don't often have to show an ID. It can be fun in charades, also. When I was a counselor as a teenager at Camp Echoing Hills in Warsaw, Ohio, a fellow counselor gave the signs for "sounds like" and "two words," then she pointed to a bruise on her leg twice. Bruise Bruise? Oh yeah, Bruce Bruce is the answer!

Uncle Reuben, by the way, is the guy who gave me a haircut when I was in kindergarten. He cut my hair short and shaved a small bald spot on the back of my head. My mother wouldn't let me go to school until the bald spot grew out again.

Of all my brothers and sisters (six in all), I am the only transplant to Athens, Ohio. I was born in Newark, Ohio, and have lived all around Southeastern Ohio. However, I moved to Athens to go to Ohio University and have never left.

At OU, I never could make up my mind whether to major in English or Philosophy, so I got a Bachelor's with a double major in both areas in 1980, then I added a Master's in English in 1984 and a Master's in Philosophy in 1985. Currently, and for a long time to come, I publish a weekly humorous column titled "Wise Up!" for *The Athens NEWS* and I am an English instructor at OU.

To see my latest "Wise Up!" column, go to www.athensnews.com—then perform a search for "David Bruce."

978-0-595-37376-5
0-595-37376-3